Anonymus

How to use Florence knitting silk

Anonymus

How to use Florence knitting silk

ISBN/EAN: 9783742833952

Manufactured in Europe, USA, Canada, Australia, Japa

Cover: Foto ©Lupo / pixelio.de

Manufactured and distributed by brebook publishing software
(www.brebook.com)

Anonymus

How to use Florence knitting silk

HOW TO USE

⇻ FLORENCE ⇺

KNITTING SILK.

FLORENCE, MASS.

NONOTUCK SILK CO.

BOSTON:
WRIGHT & POTTER PRINTING COMPANY,
18 Post Office Square.
1885.

INTRODUCTION.

I N publishing the sixth edition of our popular works on knitting, we use engravings made on a smaller scale than those illustrating previous editions, and by a more compact arraugement of type work we are enabled not only to furnish our readers with nearly all the valuable matter of earlier numbers, but with much that is new and useful, comprising a most comprehensive collection 'of rules for Mittens, Stockings, Laces, and fancy designs relating to this subject.

It is not our purpose to offer instruction in the first steps of the art of knitting, as we assume that those who will seek guidance from the pages of these books will have already advanced beyond that point in their domestic education. We advise those who have never received the primary lessons in knitting to learn at once from some friend, and thereby realize that it is a recreation that may be indulged in and enjoyed at any moment when rest from more laborious work is required.

With the issue of this collection we shall cease to publish the series known as Nos. 1, 2, 3, 4 and 5.

HINTS TO PURCHASERS OF KNITTING SILK.

The title of this book indicates the name of the silk you require for the best work with these instructions.

Florence Knitting Silk is made of the best quality of *pure* silk the market affords, prepared by combing in a manner similar to that adopted in the preparation of fine wools when intended for knitting purposes. It is *only* in this way that the peculiar " soft finish," so noticeable in all silk threads bearing the *Florence* brand, is obtained. Silk knitting yarns made by combing are *very uniform in size.* They have a *rich subdued lustre*, which is fully preserved, and even increased, by frequent washings. It is our purpose to offer the *Florence* Silk in no shade which will not bear reasonable washing without impairing its beauty of color.

Florence Knitting Silk is always sold in one-half ounce balls. It is made in two sizes: No. 300 (coarse) and No. 500 (fine). In buying see that the brand FLORENCE is plainly stamped in one end of the wood on which the silk is wound. Both sizes can be obtained in any of the following colors, viz.   black; cardinal; scarlet;

sultan; light, medium and dark garnet; pink; flesh; terra-cotta; light and medium blue; French blue; medium and dark navy; light, medium and peacock blue; turquoise blue; cadet blue; straw; bright yellow; gold; old gold; blue white; cream white; tan; fawn; drab; steel; slate; gray; light, medium and dark brown; seal brown; olive brown; invisible green; olive green in five shades; royal purple; lavender; pearl and cherry. The No. 300 size can also be had in shaded olive, scarlet, blue, yellow, brown and green.

We mention below a few of the many elegant articles which may be cheaply made of this silk, and the approximate quantity required for each, viz.:

	Ounces.		Ounces.
Gents' Half Hose,	2½	Baby's Socks,	¼
Ladies' Stockings, small,	3	Baby's Hood, crocheted or knitted,	
Ladies' Stockings, large,	4	according to size, from ½ to 1	
Ladies' Mittens,	1 to 1½	Baby's Sack, crocheted or knitted,	2
Gents' Mittens,	1½	Purse, crocheted or knitted,	¼
Wristers,	½	Skating Caps,	2

Edgings, according to width and weight; see rules for same.

NOTE.—No directions are given in this work for either hoods, sacks or caps. Many of our readers are familiar, doubtless, with methods for producing these articles in fine wool yarns, and the same methods may be adopted with our silk of similar size. Hoods, when crocheted of No. 500 Florence Knitting Silk and nicely lined with satin, are *warm*, elegant and durable.

CAUTION.

Ladies are cautioned against *all imitations of* FLORENCE KNITTING SILK, **but** more particularly those having a high gloss, as, notwithstanding their attractive surface appearance, they are invariably uneven in size, hard and wiry in finish, and lose most of their lustre, and often their color, in the first wash.

These imitations are offered by makers of sewing silk who have neither the *experience* nor the *machinery* required for making *genuine* knitting silk. Our readers, if using any of the nondescript yarns, or so-called knitting silks which we caution them against, although otherwise following the rules laid down in this book, will have no one to blame but themselves, if they meet with failure in trying to do good work. To do *good work*, one must have the *best silk*. To obtain the *best*, buy only the FLORENCE Knitting Silk. *Brilliancy* and *durability of color*, *smoothness* and *evenness* of size in thread, with softness of finish and *freedom* from all deleterious dyestuffs, are the qualities which have established the reputation of the FLORENCE, as the only Knitting Silk which has met with favorable consideration. It is for sale by dealers in fine fancy goods everywhere. Ask for it, and do not allow substitutes to be imposed upon you.

WASHING.

In washing articles made from Florence Silk, use a moderate amount of Castile Soap, thoroughly dissolved in tepid water. Extract the water by rolling and twisting in a coarse crash towel, after which put in good form and dry *without exposure to the sun.*

EDGINGS.

Lace edgings knit from the No. 500 (fine) silk, **are less** expensive than those knit from the No. 300 (coarse) silk.

Use No. 19 needles for No. 500 silk, and **No. 16 needles** for No. 300 silk, when knitting these trimmings.

All the rules given in this book for mittens and stockings are based upon an estimate of 16 stitches to each inch in width for No. 19 needles, with No. 300 Florence Knitting Silk, and 20 stitches to each inch in width with No. 500 Florence Knitting Silk and No. 22 needles. The calculation is for medium knitting, neither very close nor very loose.

SPECIAL NOTICE.

Casting on stitches should *not* be done with silk doubled, for that method makes a non-elastic edge for stockings or mittens, making it difficult to draw them on. A better method for silk, owing to its great strength, is to " knit on " the stitches from a single thread, thus obtaining a strong edge as elastic as other portions of the work.

To " knit on " stitches, tie a loop in the end of silk, and slip it on the left hand needle. Into this loop thrust the right hand needle, throw thread over, and form a stitch which place on the left hand needle. In this stitch form another, continuing this operation until the desired number of stitches is obtained.

In knitting either cotton or wool a *good* knitter will not join the ends of her thread by tying a knot, and with silk it should *never* be done. The ends may be joined so that no blemish will appear on the right side of the work, by lapping them three inches and knitting five stitches with double thread, leaving the ends on the wrong side. If in knitting the Florence Silk it is occasionally found to be already joined by tying, be sure to cut out the knots, and proceed in the manner recommended above. Do not cut off the ends on the back side of the work; they do no harm and are not seen.

CROCHETING.

We make no attempt to describe this useful and bewitching kind of work, but offer this suggestion to those who understand it—that Florence Knitting Silk is a material not to be overlooked in this connection. Wherever split zephyr, Shetland or other similar fine wool or worsted yarns are used for any crocheted article, such as shawls, hoods, sacks, nubias, clouds, &c., &c., not only the beauty, but the *durability* of the work is *greatly* increased by the introduction of stripes or edges (or both) of Florence Knitting Silk. If the wool be coarse use No. 300 silk, otherwise use No. 500.

EMBROIDERY, &c.

Excellent embroidery may be done with Florence Knitting Silk. It is also a superior article for fringe or tassels, as it does not untwist, as do most silks used for these purposes. In short, there are few kinds of fancy work in which this knitting silk may not be utilized with economy, and without sacrifice of beauty or durability

FANCY PATTERNS.

The fancy patterns described in this work, will be found of great value in knitting mittens or stockings. The descriptions are clear, and if strictly followed, there can be no failure to reproduce the designs, thus adding much beauty to these articles. For stockings knit in fancy stitches, either size of silk may be used with beautiful results, but greater satisfaction will doubtless be obtained by those who have the time to perform the extra work required, if the finer size (No. 500) be used. We would not, however, have our readers lose sight of the advantage to be gained in the use of the coarser size (No. 300) owing to its greater warmth, which is an important consideration in our cool climate at most seasons of the year.

It will be observed that at the bottom, and on the right hand side of many of the cuts showing sections of work in fancy stitch, there are dotted lines. These lines show where the pattern *as described* begins and leaves off. To illustrate: suppose that the perpendicular line *a* and the horizontal line *b* were extended into the cut, the point where they would intersect at right angles is the point where our description begins; and the point where the perpendicular line *c* and the horizontal line *d* would intersect at right angles, if extended into the cut is the point where our description ends. In other words, the angle of the lines *a b* marks the first stitch of the first round, and the angle of the lines *c d* the last stitch of last round.

This explanation is offered to prevent any confusion in the minds of knitters of small experience, as in many of the cuts the designs are shown repeated one or more times each way.

It will be found practical to use any of the patterns in the top of stockings, introducing the fancy work entirely around the same, or plain work may be adopted for the upper portion, and the fancy pattern may be confined to the front of ankle and the instep; in the latter case, plain work will be introduced in a portion of each round, and all those stitches used in the repetitions of the fancy design must be placed on the first and second needles, and those required for the plain portion of the work on the third needle. Then in knitting, the same instructions are to be followed (with the exception of the plain work at back of ankle and bottom of foot) in every round as laid down in the several rules.

With these suggestions, we leave our readers to discover many other uses for the numerous designs herein presented, confident that no one will be disappointed in the result, if strict attention is paid to our instructions in their use.

NONOTUCK SILK CO.,

FLORENCE, MASS.

HOW TO USE FLORENCE KNITTING SILK.

Explanation of Abbreviations and Terms used in giving Directions.

K — Means knit plain.

N — Is to narrow, and means to knit two stitches together.

P — Means to purl or seam.

PN — Means to purl or seam two stitches together.

S & B — Is to slip and bind, and means to slip one stitch, knit the next, and pass the slipped stitch over.

TTO — Means thread thrown over as if you were about to purl.

S — Is to slip the stitch off without knitting.

Round. When the work is done with four needles in a tubular web, this expression describes one circuit of the web from the first stitch of the first needle to the last stitch of the third needle inclusive.

Row. This term is made use of only when the work is done on two needles in a flat web.

Repeat. This word, following a description of round or row, means that the same work is to be done again, not only once, but throughout the round or row. In other places the word implies a repetition of all rows or rounds preceding it in that rule.

Position of Needles. The needle where the round begins we style the first; those which follow the second and third; and that needle which is out of the work (seldom referred to in our rules), we call the fourth. As they are constantly changing places, it is evident that it is the *position* of the needle, rather than the needle itself, which is spoken of.

Cast Off. This is done by knitting two stitches, passing the first one over the second, and repeating as required.

To knit a stitch crossed is to pass the needle into the stitch on the right-hand side instead of the left, the rest of the operation being the same as knitting plain.

Cast On. For explanation, see remarks under head of special notice on page 4.

[*** One or more stars are used, sometimes as a marginal reference, but more frequently they mark a point which is referred to again in the same or some other rule.]

DIRECTIONS FOR KNITTING.

RULE A.

General Directions for Knitting Mittens from Florence Knitting Silk.

The size of silk best adapted for this work is No. 300; and the proper size of needle is No. 10, although No. 18 needles, which are one size coarser, will answer.

[*Diagram showing manner of forming thumb, as referred to in directions for knitting Florence Silk Mittens. See Rule A.* EXPLANATION.—*The oblong piece* A, B, C, D, *shows section of wrist. The double lines,* a, b, c, d, *represent the purled stripes spoken of in said rule, and the dots on the margin of the triangular piece* (E) *represent the points where the increase is made to form the same. The triangular piece* (E) *is the lower portion of the thumb.*]

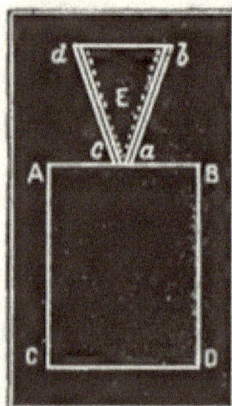

To make our instructions in the rules which will follow more easily understood, we give here some directions of a general character, which will serve to govern the knitter in making mittens of any size, either for children, for ladies, or for gentlemen.

Mittens with fancy work in wrist and back will be chiefly considered; and frequent reference will be made to diagrams. See Fig. A and Fig. AA.

These mittens are all knit in rounds, forming a tubular web, in one side of which sufficient increase is made during the progress of the work, to form a thumb. When the proper length is obtained to cover the wider portion of the hand, the web is decreased at regular intervals until all stitches are disposed of, thus giving the mittens a round finish like the toe of a stocking.

The knitting of a mitten, therefore, will be best considered in four parts: the wrist, the thumb, and the remaining portion, which for convenience we call the hand.

FIG. AA.

FIG. A.

THE WRIST.

Cast on any number of stitches which is a multiple of the number of stitches required in the fancy design to be used, and knit in rounds according to the rule laid down for the fancy pattern. Repeat the pattern any number of times to suit the length required.

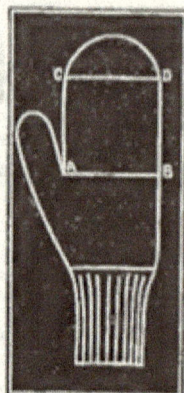

If fancy work is to be extended down the back of hand, ten or twelve rounds of plain work should be introduced both sides of the fancy stripe before the increase for thumb is begun. If fancy work is to be introduced in wrist only, the pattern should be discontinued ten or twelve rounds before the thumb is commenced, and plain knitting substituted.

In children's mittens from five to eight rounds will be enough, according to size.

POSITION OF THUMB.

In all mittens where a fancy design is introduced in the back, great care must be taken to start the thumb at such a point that the fancy stripe will be in the centre of the back of mitton *when it is on the hand*.

This will not be the case if the stripe be placed in the centre of mitten when folded as shown in Fig. **A**.

The central stitch of the fancy stripe should be about one-third the distance around the hand, measuring from the purled stripe which outlines the thumb. The number of plain stitches, therefore, between the thumb and fancy stripe, will vary according to the size of mitten and the number of stitches employed in the stripe.

It should also be remembered that on a **right-hand** mitten the thumb **must be at the left** of the fancy stripe, while on a **left-hand** mitten it must be **placed at the right** of the stripe.

Both mittens are alike where fancy work is knit only in the **wrist.**

THE THUMB.

The thumb is formed **by** taking three stitches as a base, and increasing one stitch on each of the two outside stitches, in every fourth round, until a sufficient number of stitches is obtained for the widest part.

One stitch is to be purled each side **of** the three base stitches in **every** round until the point A (Fig. **A**) is reached, thus forming purled stripes **which** outline the thumb, as shown in diagram (Fig. **AA**).

The manner of increasing is to pick up from **the** back side **of work** the loop which crosses the base of the stitch on which the increase is **made**, knit a new stitch in that loop, and *afterwards* knit the stitch itself. This method makes two stitches where there was before but one, and leaves the work solid and neat.

Another method is to pick up a loop *between* two stitches, and knit as a stitch.

Still another way is to throw the thread over, forming a loop, which becomes a new stitch in the next round. The last two methods are not recommended, as they leave small, round holes in the work, which are not desirable in a mitten. Having obtained, by increasing, the requisite number of stitches for the thumb, work **three rounds** more and place these stitches (not including the purled stitches) upon a **piece of** strong twine, and tie securely, **so** that the work may be safe while the hand is being finished. The next step **is** the formation of a small **gusset between** the thumb and hand at the point A (Fig. A), in order to make **a more perfect fit.**

THE GUSSET.

This is commenced **at the** end of the next round, by casting on four extra stitches. In the four rounds which follow, a decrease of one stitch in each round must be made at the point where the extra stitches were cast on, thus disposing of the four extra stitches, and forming one-half of a small diamond-shaped gusset, the other half being formed in the same **manner** when work on the thumb is resumed.

THE HAND.

We have already described that portion of the hand which includes the gusset, and need only add that, with the exception of the gusset, that section of work comprised between the points A, B, C, D (Fig. A), is a simple repetition of rounds of plain or fancy knitting, as best suits the taste.

The number of stitches in the round in this section **of the mitten is always** three less than were used in commencing the wrist. **To knit that portion of the** mitten represented above the points C, D (Fig. A), **observe the following instructions:** —

Having obtained the **proper length for the** widest part of the hand, **if the** number of stitches be **not already divisible by** nine, narrow in the next round at intervals of seven stitches until the **number is** so divisible; then proceed as follows, viz. : **1st round,** knit plain; —— **2d, round** * k 7, n, repeat to * and **knit 7** rounds plain; ——**10th round,** * **k** 6, n, repeat to * and knit 6 rounds **plain;** —— **17th round,** * k 5, n, repeat to * and knit 5 rounds plain; —— **23d round,** * **k** 4, n, repeat to * and knit 4 rounds plain; ——**now** narrow once on each **needle,** in every round, until only four stitches are left on a needle; then narrow **twice on** each needle and cast off. When decreasing once on each needle only, do **not narrow at the same** point **in** every round, **but** at a different place in each successive round.

TO FINISH THE THUMB.

Place the stitches which are on the **twine on three needles, and pick up 4 loops** from the base of gore formed between the hand and thumb by casting on the **4 extra** stitches. Knit once around, and narrow once in **each of the next 4 rounds at the** point where the gusset is, then knit as many **rounds as necessary to give** proper length and finish by narrowing once on each **needle in every round, until** all the stitches are disposed of.

——

RULE B.

CHILDREN'S SILK MITTENS.

There are so many sizes required **to suit** different ages, that **we** will **not undertake** to instruct as to any particular size. A general method **of** knitting mittens of all sizes **is** given in Rule A ; **but** to assist our readers further, we give the following table **as an** approximation **of** the number of stitches which will produce mittens suitable **for** various ages :

For a child of one year, 56 **stitches.**
For a child of two years, 60 **stitches.**
For a child of four years, 64 **stitches.**
For a child of six years, 70 **stitches.**

The number of stitches used, however, must be a multiple of the number required for the fancy pattern adopted; and for this reason small patterns are more desirable than large.

Fig. 33, Fig. 34, Fig. 40 or Fig. 41, are well adapted for this purpose.

The pattern used can be repeated to suit the fancy of the knitter. One-half ounce of No. 300 Florence Knitting Silk is sufficient for a pair of infant's mittens; but for the larger sizes, two balls will have to be purchased, though a portion of the second ball will not be used. We recommend a narrow hem, as described in Rule C, for these mittens.

RULE I.

LADIES' FANCY SILK MITTENS. (Fig. 1.)

MATERIALS : 1½ oz. No. 300 Florence Knitting Silk, and four No. 19 Knitting Needles.

Cast on to each of two needles 24 stitches, and on to the third needle 32 stitches, making 80 in all, and knit five rounds plain. **6th round,** n, tto, repeat.——Knit 7 rounds plain.——**14th round,** k 1, tto, k 2, s 1 k 2 together pass s over, k 2, tto, repeat.——Knit 2 rounds plain.——**17th, 20th and 23d rounds like the 14th.**——Intermediate rounds, knit plain.——Knit 2 rounds plain.——**26th round,** k 2, tto, k 1, s 1 k 2 together pass s over, k 1, tto, k 1, repeat.——Knit 2 rounds plain——**29th round,** k 3, tto, s 1 k 2 together pass s over, tto, k 2, repeat.——Knit 2 rounds plain.——**32d, 35th, 38th, 41st, 44th, 47th, 50th, 53d, 56th, 59th, 62d and 65th rounds like the 14th.**——Intermediate rounds, knit plain.——**66th and 67th rounds,** knit plain.

This completes the fancy portion of the wrist up to the point where the fancy stripe for the back of the hand begins. This stripe requires 29 stitches to knit, and each of the 12 patterns of which it is composed is complete in 8 rounds, knit as follows, viz.: **1st round,** s & b, k 6, tto, k 2, tto, k 3, s 1 k 2 together pass s over, k 3, tto, k 2, tto, k 6, n.——**2d round,** s & b, k 5, tto, k 15, tto, k 5, n.——**3d round,** s & b, k 4, tto, k 4, tto, k 3, s 1 k 2 together pass s over, k 3, tto, k 4, tto, k 4, n.——**4th round,** s & b, k 3, tto, k 19, tto, k 3, n.——**5th round,** s & b, k 2, tto, k 6, tto, k 3, s 1 k 2 together pass s over, k 3, tto, k 6, tto, k 2, n.——**6th round,** s & b, k 1, tto, k 23, tto, k 1, n.——**7th round,** s & b, tto, k3, tto, k 3, s 1 k 2 together pass s over, k 3, tto, k 3, tto, n.——**8th round,** k 29

After repeating these eight rounds twelve times, the fancy end of stripe

FIG. 1.

is knit on the same 29 stitches in six rounds, as follows, viz.: **1st round,** k 8, n, tto, k 1, tto, k 2, s 1 k 2 together pass s over, k 2, tto, k 1, tto, s & b, k 8.—— **2d round,** knit plain.—— **3d round,** k 12, tto, k 1, s 1 k 2 together pass s over, k 1, tto, k 12. —— **4th round,** knit plain.—— 5th round, k 13, tto, s 1 k 2 together pass s over, k 13.—— 6th round, knit plain. All other portions of this mitten are in plain knitting (see general directions, Rule A), and no attempt is made here at further directions, except to describe the manner of lining the wrist and open work in back. The lining is done by picking up on three needles the 80 loops formed by casting on in the beginning, and knitting as stitches in plain rounds until you have a tubular web of length to cover and form a lining to the fancy work in wrist. The first five rounds of the mitten are turned in and counted as part of the lining, the sixth forming the fancy notched edge of wrist (see engraving). Having the proper length for lining the wrist, cast off very loosely a portion of the stitches, leaving enough with which to knit a *flat* web of width and length enough to a little more than cover and form a lining to the fancy work in back of the mitten. This should be knit in rows like the heel of a stocking. When the proper length is obtained cast off *very loosely*, and finish the mitten by sewing in such a manner as will not interfere with its elasticity at the wrist. If the lining is omitted, the first five rounds of the mitten will be turned under and sewed down for a hem. This makes a neat and strong border; but a better method, where a mitten is *not* lined, is to form a hem at the commencement, as described in Rule C. We advise every lady, however, to line her mittens, as she will be amply repaid for the extra time and expense in so doing. The thumb in this mitten is commenced in the **76th round.** The mittens must be knit as "rights and lefts." **The** central stitch (that is the 15th) in the fancy design in back is the same as the *first* stitch of the pattern in wrist. If this adjustment be observed, **the** harmony of the two designs **will be perfect.** Eighty stitches at wrist makes a mitten **of size** No. 6¼ to No. **7, with medium** knitting.

—

RULE C.

DIRECTIONS FOR KNITTING A HEM.

Very attractive borders for mittens or stockings are easily made by casting on the stitches loosely and knitting several rounds plain, followed by one round of open-work knit thus: n, tto, repeat.

Follow the round of open-work with a number of rounds of plain knitting equal to that which preceded it.

In the next round, turn the edge of work up inside, and pick up and knit with each stitch on the needles one loop from the edge where your work was commenced, thus forming a perfect hem. There will always be exactly the same number of loops on the edge of the work as there are stitches on the needles, if the casting on has been properly done.

These hems may be of any desired width. In our rules for mittens we have used some narrow and some wide borders.

The knitted hem is recommended for beginning stockings either for ladies or children. It forms a neat, strong border, precisely like that seen in expensive, "full-fashioned," French hosiery, and looks much better than the ancient method of ribbing.

RULE 2.

LADIES' FANCY SILK MITTENS. (Fig. 2.)

Materials: 1½ oz. No. 300 Florence Knitting Silk, and four No. 19 knitting needles.

Cast on to each of three needles 26 stitches making 78 in all, and knit five rounds plain. 6th round, n, tto. Repeat.

Knit 7 rounds plain and commence the fancy portion of wrist by following directions given in Rule 3 (Fig. 3), which, being in thirteens, will require six repetitions for a round. This design is knit ten times for the wrist. In the next round, after the completion of the tenth repetition of the pattern, the fancy stripe for the back of mitten is commenced, and is knit by Rule 4 (Fig. 4). The pattern for this stripe requires 25 stitches, and is complete in 8 rounds. The design is knit ten times in the mitten shown here, and the finish at end of stripe is knit on the same 25 stitches, being complete in 6 rounds, as follows, viz.: 1st round, k 5, s and b, n, tto, n, tto, k 1, tto, k 1, tto, k 1, tto, n, tto, n, s and b, k 5.——2d, 3d and 4th rounds, knit plain.——5th round, k 7, s and b, n, tto, k 1, tto, k 1, tto, k 1, tto, n, s and b, k 7. ——6th round, knit plain.

The thumb is commenced in the 72d round. For manner of forming thumb and finishing hand, see Rule A. This mitten is lined in wrist and back, as described in Rule 1, with medium knitting. Seventy-eight stitches at wrist makes a mitten of size No. 6¼ to 6¾.

FIG. 2.

RULE 3.

FANCY PATTERN. (Fig. 3.)

This design is in thirteens, is knit on four needles and is complete in 5 rounds. 1st round, s 1, k 2 together, pass s over, tto, n, tto, k 1, tto, k 1, tto, k 1, tto, n, tto, k 3 together, repeat.——2d, 3d, 4th and 5th rounds, knit plain.

NOTE.—This design is used in the wrist of mitten, as shown in Fig. 2 and described in Rule 2.

The hemmed edge which appears in the cut is not included in above directions but is described in Rule 2.

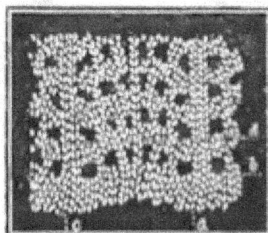

FIG. 3.

RULE 4.

FANCY PATTERN. (Fig. 4.)

Twenty-five stitches are required for this design. It is knit on four needles, and is complete in 8 rounds. 1st round, s and b, k 3, tto, s and b, n, tto, n, tto, k 1, tto, k 1, tto, k 1, tto, n, tto, n, s and b, tto, k 3, n.——2d round, knit plain.——3d round, s and b, k 2, tto, k 17, tto, k 2, n.——4th round, knit plain.——5th round, s and b, k 1, tto, k 2, s and b, n, tto, n, tto, k 1, tte, k 1, tto, k 1, tto, n, tto, n, s and b, k 2, tto, k 1, n.——6th round, knit plain.——7th round, s and b, tto, k 21, tto, n.——8th round, knit plain.

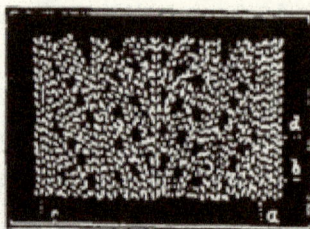

NOTE.— This design is used in the back of mitten, as shown in Fig. 2 and described in Rule 2.

FIG. 4.

RULE 5.

LADIES' FANCY SILK MITTENS. (Fig. 5.)

Materials: 1¼ ounces No. 300 Florence Knitting Silk, and four No. 19 knitting needles.

Cast on to each of two needles 30 stitches, and on to the third needle 20 stitches, making 80 stitches in all, and knit five rounds plain. 6th round, n, tto, repeat.——Knit seven rounds plain, and commence the fancy portion of wrist by following directions given in Rule 6 (Fig. 6), which, being in fives, will require sixteen repetitions for a round. This design is knit five times for the wrist. The next 21 rounds are knit in ribs, alternating 2 stitches knit plain and 2 stitches purled. 22 stitches are required for the fancy stripe in back of this mitten, which is knit according to directions given in Rule 7 (Fig. 7).

The design is knit eleven times, and the stripe is finished in eight rounds, as follows, viz.: 1st round, k 5, s and b, k 3, tto, p 2, tto, k 3, n, k 5.——2d round, k 10, p 2, k 10.——3d round, k 5, s and b, k 2, tto, k 1, p 2, k 1, tto, k 2, n, k 5.——4th round, k 10, p 2, k 10.——5th round, k 5, s and b, k 1, tto, k 2, p 2, k 2, tto, k 1, n, k 5.——6th round, k 10, p 2, k 10.——7th round, k 5, s and b, tto, k 3, p 2, k 3, tto, n, k 5.——8th round, k 10, p 2, k 10. The thumb is commenced in the 84th round of the wrist, which is of extra length. For manner of forming thumb and finishing hand, see Rule A.

This mitten is lined in wrist and back, in the same way as described in Rule 1. Eighty stitches at wrist makes a mitten of size No. 6½ to No. 7, with medium knitting.

FIG. 5.

RULE 6.

FANCY PATTERN. (Fig. 6.)

This design is in fives, is knit on four needles, and is complete in 8 rounds. 1st round, tto, k 3, n, repeat.——2d round, knit plain.——3d round, k 1, tto, k 2, n, repeat.——4th round, knit plain. —— 5th round, k 2, tto, k 1, n, repeat.—— 6th round, knit plain. —— 7th round, k 3, tto, n, repeat.—— 8th round, knit plain.

NOTE.—This design is used in the wrist of mitten, as shown in Fig. 5, and described in Rule 5.

The hemmed edge which appears in the cut, is not included in above directions, but is described in Rule 5.

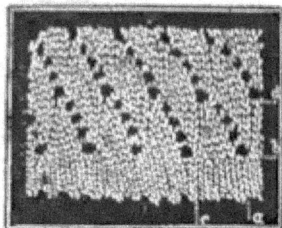

FIG. 6.

RULE 7.

FANCY PATTERN. (Fig. 7.)

Twenty-two stitches are required for this design. It is knit on four needles, and is complete in 8 rounds. 1st round, s and b, k 3, tto, s and b, k 3, tto, p 2, tto, k 3, n, tto, k 3, n. —— 2d round, k 10, p 2, k 10.—— 3d round, s and b, k 2, tto, k 1, s and b, k 2, tto, k 1, p 2, k 1, tto, k 2, n, k 1, tto, k 2, n.——4th round, k 10, p 2, k 10. —— 5th round, s and b, k 1, tto, k 2, s and b, k 1, tto, k 2, p 2, k 2, tto, k 1, n, k 2, tto, k 1, n. —— 6th round, k 10, p 2, k 10. —— 7th round, s and b, tto, k 3, s and b, tto, k 3, p 2, k 3, tto, n, k 3, tto, n.——8th round, k 10, p 2, k 10.

NOTE.—This design is used in the back of mitten, as shown in Fig. 5, and described in Rule 5.

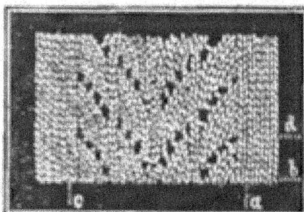

FIG. 7.

RULE 8.

LADIES' FANCY SILK MITTENS. (Fig. 8.)

Materials : 1¾ oz. No. 300 Florence Knitting Silk, and four No. 19 knitting needles.

FIG. 8.

Cast on to each of three needles 27 stitches, making 81 stitches in all, and knit five rounds plain. 6th round, n, tto, repeat, ending round with k 1, to dispose of odd stitch. Knit seven rounds plain, and commence the fancy portion of wrist by following directions given in Rule 9 (Fig 9), which, being in nines, will require nine repetitions for a round. This design is knit eight times for the wrist. 27 stitches are required for the fancy stripe in the back of this mitten, consisting of three repetitions of the design in wrist. These three repetitions are knit fourteen times, and the finish at end of stripe is knit on the same 27 stitches, being complete in 6 rounds, as follows, viz.: **1st round,** k 5, tto, k 2, n, s and b, k 2, tto, k 1, tto, k 2, n, s and b, k 2, tto, k 5. —— **2d round,** knit plain. —— **3d round,** k 6, tto, k 1, n, s and b, k 1, tto, k 3, tto, k 1, n, s and b, k 1, tto, k 6. —— **4th round,** knit plain. —— **5th round,** k 7, tto, n, s and b, tto, k 5, tto, n, s and b, tto, k 7. —— **6th round,** knit plain. The thumb is commenced in the **74th** round. For manner of forming thumb and finishing hand see Rule A. This mitten is lined in wrist and back in the same way as described in Rule 1. Eighty-one stitches at wrist makes a mitten of size No. 6¼ to No. 7 with medium knitting.

———

RULE 9.

FANCY PATTERN. (Fig. 9.)

This design is in nines, is knit on four needles, and is complete in six rounds.

FIG. 9.

1st round, s and b, k 2, tto, k 1, tto, k 2, n, repeat. —— **2d round,** knit plain. —— **3d round,** s and b, k 1, tto, k 3, tto, k 1, n, repeat. —— **4th round,** knit plain. —— **5th round,** s and b, tto, k 5, tto, n, repeat. —— **6th round,** knit plain.

NOTE. — This design is used in the wrist and back of mitten, as shown in Fig. 8, and described in Rule 8.

The hemmed edge which appears in the cut is not included in above directions, but is described in Rule 8.

RULE 10.

LADIES' FANCY SILK MITTENS. (Fig. 10.)

Materials : 1¼ oz. No. 300 Florence Knitting Silk, and four No. 19 knitting needles.

Cast on to each of three needles 26 stitches, making 78 stitches in all, and knit 5 rounds plain. 6th round, n, tto, repeat.—— Knit seven rounds plain, and commence the fancy portion of wrist by following directions given in Rule 11 (Fig. 11), which, being in thirteens, will require six repetitions for n round. This design is knit five times for the wrist. 26 stitches are required for the fancy stripe in the back of this mitten, consisting of two repetitions of the design in wrist. These two repetitions are knit eight times, and the finish at end of stripe is knit on the same 26 stitches, being complete in 10 rounds, as follows, viz.: 1st round, k 7, tto, k 4, n, s and b, k 4, tto, k 7.——2d round, knit plain.——3d round, k 8, tto, k 3, n, s and b, k 3, tto, k 8.——4th round, knit plain.——5th round, k 9, tto, k 2, n, s and b, k 2, tto, k 9.——6th round, knit plain.——7th round, k 10, tto, k 1, n, s and b, k 1, tto, k 10.——8th round, knit plain.——9th round, k 11, tto, n, s and b, tto, k 11.——10th round, knit plain. The thumb is commenced in the 74th round.

For manner of forming thumb and finishing hand, see Rule A. This mitten is lined in wrist and back in the same way as described in Rule 1.

Seventy-eight stitches at wrist makes a mitten of size No. 6¼ to 6¾, with medium knitting.

FIG. 10.

RULE 11.

FANCY PATTERN. (Fig. 11.)

This design is in thirteens, is knit on four needles, and is complete in 10 rounds.

1st round, s and b, k 4, tto, k 1, tto, k 4, n, repeat.——2d round, knit plain.——3d round, s and b, k 3, tto, k 3, tto, k 3, n, repeat.——4th round, knit plain.——5th round, s and b, k 2, tto, k 5, tto, k 2, n, repeat.—— 6th round, knit plain.——7th round, s and b, k 1, tto, k 7, tto, k 1, n, repeat.——8th round, knit plain.——9th round, s and b, tto, k 9, tto, n, repeat.——10th round, knit plain.

NOTE.— This design is used in the wrist and back of mitten, as shown in Fig. 10, and described in Rule 10.

FIG. 11.

The hemmed edge which appears in the cut is not included in above directions, but is described in Rule 10.

RULE 12.

LADIES' FANCY SILK MITTENS. (Fig. 12.)

Materials : 1½ oz. No. 300 Florence Knitting Silk, and four No. 19 knitting needles. *Cast on to each of two needles 30 stitches, and on to the third needle 20 stitches, making 80 in all, and knit fifteen rounds plain.* 16th round, n, tto, repeat. —— Knit 6 rounds plain. —— 23d round, tto, s and b, k 6, repeat. ——24th round, k 1, tto, s and b, k 5, repeat. —— 25th round, k 2, tto, s and b, k 4, repeat. —— 26th round, k 3, tto, s and b, k 3, repeat. —— 27th round, k 4, tto, s and b, k 2, repeat. ——Knit five rounds plain. ——33d round, n, tto, repeat. ——34th round, knit plain. —— 35th round, k 2, tto, s and b, k 4, repeat. ——36th round, knit plain. ——37th round, k 3, tto, s and b, k 3, repeat. 38th round, knit plain. ——39th round, k 4, tto, s and b, k 2, repeat. ——40th round, knit plain. 41st round, k 2, n, tto, k 1, tto, s and b, k 1, repeat. ——42d round, knit plain. ——43d round, k 1, n, tto, k 5, repeat. ——44th round, knit plain. ——45th round, n, tto, k 1, tto, s and b, k 3, repeat. ——46th round, knit plain. ——47th round, like 39th. ——48th round, knit plain. ——49th round, like 41st, —— 50th round, knit plain. ——51st round, like 43d. —— 52d round, knit plain. ——53d round, like 45th. ——54th round, knit plain. ——55th round, like 39th. ——56th round, knit plain. ——57th round, like 41st. ——58th round, knit plain. The next 21 rounds are knit in ribs, alternating 2 stitches knit plain and 2 stitches purled.

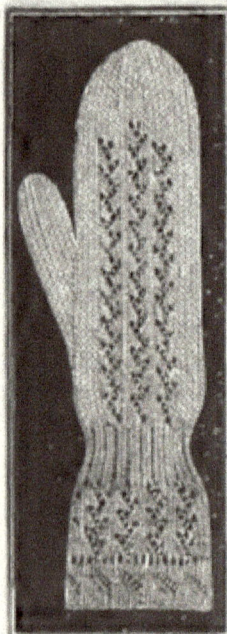

FIG. 12.

The fancy stripe in back consists of three repetitions of the design described in Rule 13 (Fig. 13). This design being in eights, will require 24 stitches. It is knit ten times to form the stripe; the first 4 rounds, however, being *always* omitted after the beginning. The stripe is finished after the tenth repetition of the pattern, on the same 24 stitches, in twelve rounds as follows, viz.: 1st round, k 4, tto, s and b, k 6, tto, s and b, k 6, tto, s and b, k 2.——2d round, knit plain.——3d round, k 2, n, tto, k 1, tto, s and b, k 3, n, tto, k 1, tto, s and b, k 3, n, tto, k 1, tto, s and b, k 1.——4th round, knit plain.——5th round, k 9, n, tto, k 13.——6th round, knit plain.——7th round, k 8, n, tto, k 1, tto, s and b, k 11.——8th round, knit plain——9th round, k 12, tto, s and b, k 10. ——10th round, knit plain.——11th round, k 10, n, tto, k 1, tto, s and b, k 9.——12th round, knit plain.

The thumb is commenced in the 86th round of the wrist, which is of extra length. For manner of forming thumb and finishing hand, see Rule 1.

This mitten is lined in wrist and back in the same way as described in Rule 1.

Eighty stitches at wrist makes a mitten of size No. 6½ to No. 7, with medium knitting.

RULE 13.

FANCY PATTERN. (Fig. 13.)

This design is in eights, is knit on four needles, and is complete in 12 rounds. 1st round, k 2, tto, s and b, k 4 repeat.—2d round, knit plain.—3d round, k 3, tto, s and b, k 3, repeat.—4th round, knit plain.—5th round, k 4, tto, s and b, k 2, repeat.—6th round, knit plain.—7th round, k 2, u, tto, k 1, tto, s and b, k 1, repeat.—8th round, knit plain.—9th round, k 1, n, tto, k 5, repeat.—10th round, knit plain.—11th round, n, tto, k 1, tto, s and b, k 3, repeat.—12th round, knit plain.

NOTE.—This design is used in the wrist and back of mitten, as shown in Fig. 12, and described in Rule 12.

To repeat the pattern, omit the first four rounds. The hemmed edge which appears in the cut is not included in above directions, but is described in Rule 12.

FIG. 13.

RULE 14.

LADIES' FANCY SILK MITTENS. (Fig. 14.)

Materials: 1½ oz. No. 300 Florence Knitting Silk, and four No. 19 knitting needles.

Cast on to each of two needles 30 stitches, and on to the third needle 20 stitches, making 80 in all, and knit 15 rounds plain. 16th round, n, tto, repeat.—Knit 5 rounds plain.—22d round, k 5, tto, s and b, k 3, repeat.—23d round, knit plain.—24th round, k 3, n, tto, k 1, tto, s and b, k 2, repeat.—25th round, k 2, n, tto, k 3, tto, s and b, k 1, repeat.—26th round, k 1, n, tto, k 5, tto, s and b, repeat.—Knit 6 rounds plain.—33d round, n, tto, repeat.—34th round, knit plain.—35th round, k 5, tto, s and b, k 3, repeat.—36th round, knit plain.—37th round, k 3, n, tto, k 1, tto, s and b, k 2, repeat.—38th round, knit plain.—39th round, k 2, n, tto, k 3, tto, s and b, k 1, repeat.—40th round, knit plain.—41st round, k 1, n, tto, k 5, tto, s and b, repeat.—42d round, knit plain.—43d round, k 3, tto, s and b, k 1, n, tto, k 2.—44th round, knit plain.—45th round, k 4, tto, s 1, n, pass s over, tto, k 3.—46th round, knit plain.—47th round, like 39th.—48th round, knit plain.—49th round, like 41st.—50th round, knit plain.—51st round, like 43d.—52d round, knit plain.—53d round, like 45th.—54th round, knit plain.—55th round, like 39th.—56th round, knit plain.—57th round, like 41st.—58th round, knit plain.—59th round, like 43d.—60th round, knit plain.—61st round, like 45th.—62d round,

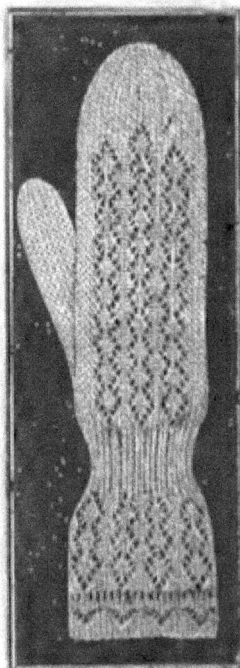

FIG. 14.

knit plain.——63d round, k 5, tto, s and b, k 3.——64th round, knit plain. The next 21 rounds are knit in ribs alternating 2 stitches knit plain and 2 stitches purled.

The fancy stripe in back consists of three repetitions of the design described in Rule 15 (Fig. 15). This design being in tens will require 30 stitches. It is knit ten times to form the stripe, the *first* 4 rounds, however, being always omitted after the beginning. The stripe is finished after the tenth repetition of the pattern, on the same 30 stitches in 10 rounds, as follows, viz.: 1st round, k 4, n, tto, k 6, n, tto, k 3, tto, s and b, k 6, tto, s and b, k 3.——2d round, knit plain.——3d round, k 11, n, tto, k 5, tto, s and b, k 10.——4th round, knit plain.——5th round, k 13, tto, s and b, k 1, n, tto, k 12.——6th round, knit plain.——7th round, k 14, tto, s 1, n, pass s over, tto, k 13.——8th round, knit plain.——9th round, k 14, n, tto, k 14.——10th round, knit plain.

The thumb is commenced in the **94th round** of the wrist, which is of extra length.

For manner of forming thumb and finishing hand (see Rule **A**).

This mitten is lined in wrist and back, in the same way as described in Rule 1.

Eighty stitches at wrist makes a mitten of size No. 6½ to No. 7, with medium knitting

—

RULE 15.

FANCY PATTERN. (Fig. 15.)

This design is in tens, is knit on four needles, and is complete in 12 rounds. 1st round, k 5, tto, s and b, k 3, repeat.——2d round, knit plain.——3d round, k 3, n, tto, k 1, tto, s and b, k 2, repeat.——4th round, knit plain.——5th round, k 2, n, tto, k 3, tto, s and b, k 1, repeat.——6th round, knit plain.——7th round, k 1, n, tto, k 5, tto, s and b, repeat.——8th round, knit plain.——9th round, k 3, tto, s and b, k 1, n, tto, k 2, repeat.——10th round, knit plain.——11th round, k 4, tto, s 1, n, pass s over, tto, k 3, repeat.——12th round, knit plain.

NOTE.——This design is used in the wrist and back of mitten, as shown in Fig. 14, and described in Rule 14.

To repeat the pattern, omit the first 4 rounds. The hemmed edge which appears in the cut is not included in above directions, but is described in Rule 14.

FIG. 15.

RULE 16.

LADIES' FANCY SILK MITTENS. (Fig. 16.)

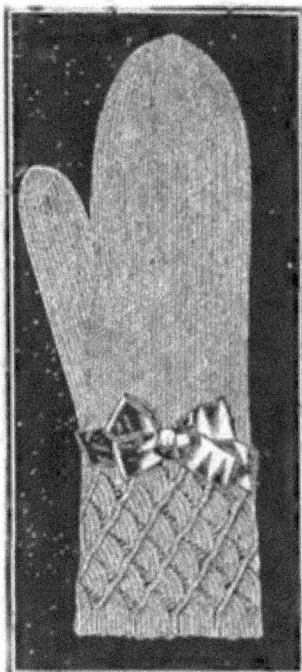

Materials: 1½ oz. No. 300 Florence Knitting Silk, and four No. 19 knitting needles.

Cast on 80 stitches, and knit 6 rounds plain. **7th round,** n, tto, repeat.——Knit 6 rounds plain and commence the fancy portion of wrist by following directions given in Rule 17 (Fig. 17), which being in eights will require ten repetitions for a round. The design is knit six times for the wrist.

After the fancy work is complete, knit ten rounds plain before commencing thumb.

For manner of forming thumb and finishing hand, see Rule A.

This mitten is lined in wrist, in the same way as described in Rule 1.

Eighty stitches at wrist makes a mitten of size No. 6½ to No. 7, with medium knitting.

FIG. 16.

RULE 17.

FANCY PATTERN. (Fig. 17.)

This design is in eights, is knit on four needles, and is complete in 7 rounds. **1st round,** tto, k 6, n, repeat.——**2d round,** k 1, tto, k 5, n, repeat.——**3d round,** k 2, tto, k 4, n, repeat.——**4th round,** k 3, tto, k 3, n, repeat.——**5th round,** k 4, tto, k 2, n, repeat. ——**6th round,** k 5, tto, k 1, n, repeat.—— **7th round,** k 6, tto, n, repeat.

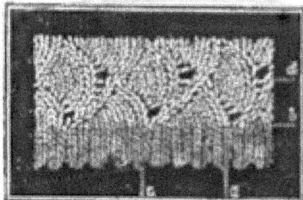

NOTE.—This design is used in the wrist of mitten, as shown in Fig. 16 and described in Rule 16.

FIG. 17.

The hemmed edge which appears in the cut is not included in above directions, but is described in Rule 18.

RULE 18.

LADIES' FANCY SILK MITTENS. (Fig. 18.)

Materials: 1½ oz. No. 300 Florence Knitting Silk and four No. 19 knitting needles.

Cast on to each of two needles 25 stitches, and on to the third needle 30 stitches, making 80 in all, and knit 5 rounds plain. 6th round, n, tto, repeat. —— Knit 7 rounds plain. —— 14th round, tto, k 3, n, repeat. —— 15th, 16th, 17th, 18th, 19th, 20th and 21st rounds, like 14th. —— Knit 8 rounds plain. —— 30th round, tto, k 6, n, repeat. —— 31st round, k 1, tto, k 5, n, repeat. —— 32d round, k 2, tto, k 4, n, repeat. —— 33d round, k 3, tto, k 3, n, repeat. —— 34th round, k 4, tto, k 2, n, repeat. —— 35th round, k 5, tto, k 1, n, repeat. —— 36th round, k 6, tto, n, repeat. —— 37th round, knit plain. The last eight rounds are repeated five times to complete the pattern in wrist. The fancy stripe in back of hand requires 29 stitches. There are nine repetitions of the pattern knit in 8 rounds each as follows, viz.: 1st round, s and b, k 6, tto, k 2, tto, k 3, s 1, n, pass s over, k 3, tto, k 2, tto, k 6, n. —— 2d round, s and b, k 5, tto, k 15, tto, k 5, n. —— 3d round, s and b, k 4, tto, k 4, tto, k 3, s 1, n, pass s over, k 3, tto, k 4, tto, k 4, n. —— 4th round, s and b, k 3, tto, k 19, tto, k 3, n. —— 5th round, s and b, k 2, tto, k 6, tto, k 3, s 1, n, pass s over, k 3, tto, k 6, tto, k 2, n. —— 6th round, s and b, k 1, tto, k 23, tto, k 1, n. —— 7th round, s and b, tto, k 8, tto, k 3, s 1, n, pass s over, k 3, tto, k 8, tto, n. —— 8th round, k 29.

The fancy design at end of stripe is knit on the same 29 stitches in 41 rounds, as follows, viz.: 1st round, k 1, s and b, k 5, tto, k 2, tto, k 3, s 1, n, pass s over, k 3, tto, k 2, tto, k 5, n, k 1. 2d round, k 1, s and b, k 4, tto, k 15, tto, k 4, n, k 1. —— 3d round, k 1, s and b, k 3, tto, k 4, tto, k 3, s 1, n, pass s over, k 3, tto, k 4, tto, k 3, n, k 1. —— 4th round, k 1, s and b, k 2, tto, k 19, tto, k 2, n, k 1. —— 5th round, k 1, s and b, k 1, tto, k 6, tto, k 3, s 1, n, pass s over, k 3, tto, k 6, tto, k 1, n, k 1. —— 6th round, k 1, s and b, tto, k 23, tto, n, k 1. —— 7th round, k 10, tto, k 3, s 1, n, pass s over, k 3, tto, k 10. —— 8th round, k 2, s and b, k 4, tto, k 13, tto, k 4, n, k 2. —— 9th round, k 2, s and b, k 3, tto, k 3, tto, k 3, s 1, n, pass s over, k 3, tto, k 3, tto, k 3, n, k 2. —— 10th

FIG. 18.

round, k 2, s and b, k 2, tto, k 17, tto, k 2, n, k 2.——11th round, k 2, s and b, k 1, tto, k 5, tto, k 3, s 1, n, pass s over, k 3, tto, k 5, tto, k 1, n, k 2.——12th round, k 2, s and b, tto, k 21, tto, n, k 2.——13th round, like 7th.——14th round, k 3, s and b, k 3, tto, k 13, tto, k 3, n, k 3.——15th round, k 3, s and b, k 2, tto, k 3, tto, k 3, s 1, n, pass s over, k 3, tto, k 3, tto, k 2, n, k 3.——16th round, k 3, s and b, k 1, tto, k 17, tto, k 1, n, k 3.——17th round, k 3, s and b, k 5, tto, k 3, s 1, n, pass s over, k 3, tto, k 5, tto, n, k 3.——18th round, k 29.——19th round, k 4, s and b, k 3, tto, k 11, tto, k 3, n, k 4.——20th round, k 4, s and b, k 2, tto, k 3, tto, k 2, s 1, n, pass s over, k 2, tto, k 3, tto, k 2, n, k 4.——21st round, k 4, s and b, k 1, tto, k 15, tto, k 1, n, k 4.——22d round, k 4, s and b, tto, k 17, tto, n, k 4.——23d round, k 12, tto, k 1, s 1, n, pass s over, k 1, tto, k 12.——24th round, k 29.——25th round, k 6, s and b, k 3, tto, k 7, tto, k 3, n, k 6.——26th round, k 6, s and b, k 2, tto, k 3, s 1, n, pass s over, k 3, tto, k 2, n, k 6.——27th round, k 6, s and b, k 1, tto, k 11, tto, k 1, n, k 6.——28th round, k 6, s and b, tto, k 13, tto, n, k 6.——29th round, k 29.——30th round, k 7, s and b, k 3, tto, k 5, tto, k 3, n, k 7.——31st round, k 7, s and b, k 2, tto, k 7, tto, k 2, n, k 7.——32d round, k 7, s and b, k 1, tto, k 9, tto, k 1, n, k 7.——33d round, k 7, s and b, tto, k 11, tto, n, k 7.——34th round, k 29.——35th round, k 9, s and b, k 3, tto, k 1, tto, k 3, n, k 9.——36th round, k 9, s and b, k 2, tto, k 3, tto, k 2, n, k 9.——37th round, k 9, s and b, k 1, tto, k 5, tto, k 1, n, k 9.——38th round, k 9, s and b, tto, k 7, tto, n, k 9.——39th round, k 29.——40th round, k 11, s and b, k 1, tto, k 1, tto, k 1, n, k 11.——41st round, k 29. All other portions of this mitten are knit plain (see general directions, Rule A). The wrist and fancy back are lined in manner described in Rule 1. The thumb is commenced in the 70th round. Eighty stitches at wrist makes a mitten of size No. 6½ to No. 7.

When shaping the tip of hand decrease only in the plain portions of the work.

RULE 19.

LADIES' SILK MITTENS. (Fig. 19.)

Materials: 1 oz. No. 300 Florence Knitting Silk, and four No. 19 knitting needles.

Cast on to each of two needles 25 stitches and on to the third needle 30 stitches, making 80 in all, and knit five rounds plain.——**6th round,** n, tto, repeat. Knit 6 rounds plain.——**13th round,** tto, k 3, n, repeat.——**14th, 15th, 16th, 17th** and **18th rounds** like 13th.

Knit 14 rounds plain. Knit 38 rounds alternating 2 stitches knit plain and two purled. The thumb is commenced in **77th round.** For further directions, see Rule **A.**

Eighty stitches at wrist makes a mitten of size No. 6½ to No. 7 with medium knitting.

FIG. 19.

RULE 20.

LADIES' FANCY SILK MITTENS. (Fig. 20.)

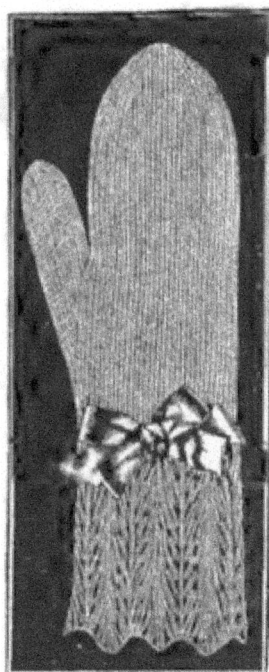

FIG. 20.

Materials: 1 oz. No. 300 Florence Knitting Silk and four No. 19 knitting needles.

Cast on 77 stitches, and knit once around plain. The fancy portion of wrist is knit by following directions given in Rule 21 (Fig. 21), which being in elevens will require seven repetitions for a round.

The design is knit twelve times for the wrist. After the fancy work is complete, knit ten rounds plain before commencing thumb.

For manner of forming thumb and finishing hand, see Rule A.

Seventy-seven stitches at wrist makes a mitten of size No. 6¼ to No. 6¾, with medium knitting.

The wrist in this mitten is not lined.

RULE 21.

FANCY PATTERN. (Fig. 21.)

This design is in elevens, is knit on four needles, and is complete in four rounds. Having cast on any number of stitches divisible by eleven, and knit one plain round, knit the pattern as follows, viz.: **1st round,** n, n, tto, k 1, tto, k 1, tto, k 1, tto, n, n, repeat.——**2d, 3d and 4th rounds,** knit plain.

NOTE.—This design is used in the wrist of the mitten, as shown in Fig. 20, and described in Rule 20.

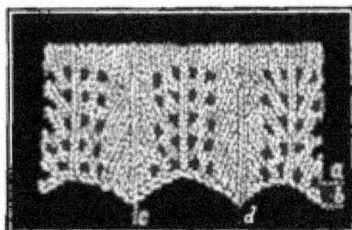

FIG. 21.

RULE 22.

LADIES' FANCY SILK MITTENS. (Fig. 22.)

Materials: 1 oz. No. 300 Florence Knitting Silk and five No. 19 knitting needles.

Cast on to each of two needles 25 stitches and on to the third needle 30 stitches, making 80 in all, and knit 5 rounds plain. **6th round,** n, tto, repeat. —— Knit 7 rounds plain. —— **14th round,** tto, k 3, n, repeat. —— **15th, 16th and 17th rounds** like 14th. —— **18th round,** knit plain. —— **19th round,** k 1, tto, s and h, k 2, repeat. —— **20th round,** k 2, tto, s and b, k 1, repeat. —— **21st round,** k 3, tto, s and h, repeat. —— Knit 15 rounds plain. —— Knit 35 rounds, alternating 3 stitches knit plain and 2 purled.

The fancy stripe in back of hand requires 29 stitches. There are 13 repetitions of the pattern knit in 8 rounds each as follows, viz.: **1st round,** p 2, slip the next 3 stitches on to the fifth or extra needle (without knitting), and, passing *back* of these 3 slipped stitches, knit the next 3 and then the 3 on the extra needle, p 2, slip 3 on extra needle, k 3 from *behind* the 3 slipped stitches, k 3 from extra needle, k 3, p 2, slip the next three on to the extra needle, and, passing in *front* of these 3 slipped stitches, knit the next 3 and then knit the 3 on the extra needle, p 2. —— **2d, 3d and 4th rounds,** p 2, k 6, p 2, k 9, p 2, k 6, p 2. —— **5th round,** p 2, k 6, p 2, k 3, slip the next 3 on to the extra needle, and, passing in *front* of these 3 slipped stitches, knit the next 3 and then knit the 3 on the extra needle, p 2, k 6, p 2. —— **6th, 7th and 8th rounds,** p 2, k 6, p 2, k 9, p 2, k 6, p 2. After the 13th repetition of the pattern, the end of stripe is knit on the same 29 stitches in 12 rounds, as follows, viz.: **1st round,** same as 1st round in the pattern just described. —— **2d round,** p 2, s 1, n, pass s over, s 1, n, pass s over, p 2, k 9, p 2, s 1, n, pass s over, s 1, n, pass s over, p 2. —— **3d round,** p 2, s and h, p 3, k 9, p 2, s and h, p 2. —— **4th round,** p 5, k 9, p 5. —— **5th round,** p 5, k 3, slip without knitting 3 stitches on extra needle, knit from *front* of the slipped stitches the

FIG. 22.

next 3 and then the 3 from extra needle, p 5.——**6th** round, p 5, k 9, p 5.——
7th round, p 5, s and b, k 5, n, p 5.——**8th round**, p 5, s and b, k 3, n, p 5.
——**9th round**, p 5, s and b, k 1, n, p 5.——**10th round, p 5, s 1, n, pass s**
over, p 5.——**11th round**, s and h, p 7, n.——**12th round**, s and b, p 5, n. All
other parts of this mitten are knit plain. (See general directions, Rule A.) The
thumb is commenced in the **78th round**. As the braid and twist patterns in back
tend to contract the work, it would be advisable to make 8 extra stitches in the first
round after ribbed work, as this pattern as described will otherwise be only suitable for a large miss wearing size No. 5½ or No. 6.

In shaping the tip of the hand, decrease only in plain portions of the work, making due allowance for decrease already made in the end of stripe.

RULE 23.

LONG SILK PURSE. (Fig. 23.)

Materials: ½ ounce size EE Corticelli Purse Twist or ½ ounce No. 300 Florence
Knitting Silk, and two No. 18 needles.

Cast on to one needle 59 stitches, knit across once
plain. **2d row, purl 2** together, tto, repeat until
only 1 stitch remains, knit 1.——**3d row** and every
row after until the **65th row** is reached, the same
as the **2d.**

Now do 83 rows of plain knitting (garter stitch),
then knit 64 rows of the fancy pattern the
same as at the beginning, knit 1 row plain and
cast off. You now have a long flat piece, a
little narrower in the centre than at the ends;
sew up the edges, leaving an opening of 2½
inches on one side; finish with steel trimmings.

In knitting this purse care must be taken to
keep up the number of stitches, as one may
be easily dropped and not noticed. In commencing each row there must always be 59
stitches on the needle.

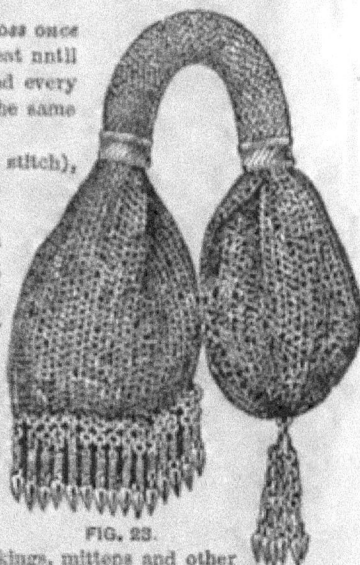

FIG. 23.

NOTE.— Corticelli Purse Twist is put up
on long black spools, each containing ½ ounce
of hard twisted silk, better adapted for purse
work than the Knitting Silk, which for stockings, mittens and other
articles which require washing should be of slack twist and "*soft finish*," thus
securing greater elasticity and durability.

The Knitting Silk, however, **makes an** excellent purse, and costs less than the
purse silk, which requires more labor in its preparation.

RULE 24.

LADIES' SILK PURSE. (Fig. 24.)

Materials: ½ ounce Corticelli Purse Twist, size EE, and four No. 18 knitting needles.

Begin knitting with two needles only. Leave hanging an end of silk ten inches long, for over-seaming the trimmings, and cast on 20 stitches. Knit across in rows (style called garter stitch, that is, all rows are knit and none purled), five times. **6th row,** k 3, tto, k 14, tto, k 3.——**7th row,** k 22.——**8th row,** k 3, tto, k 16, tto, k 3.——**9th row,** k 24.——**10th row,** k 3, tto, k 16, tto, k 3.——**11th row,** k 26.——**12th row,** k 3, tto, k 20, tto, k 3.——**13th row,** k 28.——**14th row,** k 3, tto, k 22, tto, k 3.——**15th row,** k 30.——**16th row,** k 3, tto, k 24, tto, k 3.——**17th row,** k 32.——**18th row,** k 3, tto, k 26, tto, k 3.——**19th row,** k 34.——**20th row,** k 3, tto, k 28, tto, k 3.——**21st row,** k 36. Cut the silk, leaving an end hanging about 10 inches long. Cast on to another needle 20 stitches and knit a second piece in 21 rows as above, but do not break silk. This completes the two flat pieces of web which form the mouth of the purse. Transfer 12 stitches from each needle to a third needle and begin knitting in rounds, as follows; viz., knit 6 rounds plain.——**7th round,** n, tto, repeat. Knit 5 rounds plain.——**13th round,** k 3, tto, s 1, n, pass s over, tto, k 2, repeat.——**14th, 16th and 18th rounds, knit plain.——**

FIG. 24.

15th round, k 1, n, tto, k 3, tto, s and b, repeat.——17th round, like the 13th. Knit 2 rounds plain. Transfer the first 4 stitches on each needle to the next needle, thereby leaving 4 stitches on the third needle to be considered as part of the 20th round, and knit as such in addition to the stitches already disposed of.——21st and 25th rounds, like 13th.——22d, 24th and 26th rounds, knit plain. ——23d round, like 15th.——27th round, knit plain.——28th round, knit all plain but last 4 stitches, then transfer the last 4 stitches on each needle to next needle and consider the 28th round complete.——29th and 33d rounds, like 13th.——30th, 32d and 34th rounds, knit plain.——31st round, like 15th. Knit 2 rounds plain.

Transfer the first four stitches on each needle to the next needle, thereby leaving four stitches on the third needle to be considered as part of the 36th round and knit as such in addition to the stitches already disposed of. 37th and 41st rounds, like 13th.——38th, 40th and 42d rounds, knit plain.——39th round, like 15th.——Knit 5 rounds plain.——48th round, n, tto, repeat.—— Knit 6 rounds plain.——55th round, k 4, n, repeat.——Knit 2 rounds plain.—— 58th round, k 3, n, repeat.——Knit 2 rounds plain.——61st round, k 2, n, repeat. ——Knit 2 rounds plain.——64th round, k 1, n, repeat.——Knit 1 round plain and narrow twice in every round thereafter until all the stitches are disposed of but six, then cast off leaving an end of silk which is to be afterwards used, not only to secure stitches, but at same time to sew on the metallic ornament at bottom of purse. The bag is now to be turned inside out, as what is termed the purled side of the knitting is the outside as shown in the engraving, although if the worker prefers, the other side may be used. With the ends of silk left hanging where the stitches were cast on, and a coarse needle, secure one of the metal bars to each edge, passing the threaded needle over the bar, and through each and every loop at the top of the purse, thus forming an extremely elegant and durable finish. Fasten at corner neatly and securely and cut off ends and you have a purse knit without any necessity for tying a knot at any point in the work.

One-half ounce of Corticelli Silk will make two of these purses.

The engraving shows purse in full size.

The steel trimmings can be obtained at the best fancy goods stores.

FLORENCE SILK HOSIERY,

FOR LADIES.

These goods are manufactured from fine **FLORENCE KNITTING SILK**, on hand frames, in the best "full-fashioned" shapes known to the trade.

They are made extra long, are dyed in the yarn, and may be washed without injury to colors.

Being heavier than most silk hose, they are adapted for winter use, either for invalids or persons who wish to avoid becoming such.

Purchasers should notice our trade-mark (**F**) knitted into the hem at the top of each stocking in all our best hosiery for ladies.

NONOTUCK SILK CO.

STOCKINGS.

RULE D.

General Directions for ascertaining the number of Stitches needed for knitting Stockings from Florence Knitting Silk.

As much variation exists in the style of work done by different persons, some knitting loose and others very close, it is not practical to give an exact number of stitches which will answer for any given size of stockings; but the following rule will enable any one to estimate in each case the number of stitches required :—

Select the size of silk and needles you design using, cast about 25 stitches on to one needle and knit, say twenty times across, back and forth, in the same manner as for the heel of a stocking.

Now lay a measure on the sample piece of knitting so obtained, and count the number of stitches to one inch in width; next select a cotton stocking of good shape and proper size, lay it flat upon a table and measure across the top, just below the hem, if woven, and just below the seamed part, if hand-knit.

This measurement will be one-half the number of inches around the stocking leg in the largest part. Having found the number of stitches to the inch of your work, and the number of inches your stocking measures, multiply the two together, and the product is the whole number of stitches necessary to knit a stocking from Florence Knitting Silk of the same size as your cotton pattern.

To illustrate : **If your** sample counts 16 stitches to the inch, and your pattern stocking **measures** 10½ inches around, then it follows that the whole number of stitches **needed is** 168. The silk used in knitting the sample piece need not be **wasted, as it can be** ravelled and knit again.

RULE E.

GENTS' SILK SOCKS.

Materials : 2½ ounces No. 300 FLORENCE Knitting Silk, and four No. 19 knitting needles.

Cast 113 stitches on three needles, knit once around plain, then knit in ribs, alternating 4 stitches plain and 2 purl, 70 rounds, which will give about 3½ inches; then knit plain 6 inches, and commence heel by taking 57 stitches on one needle, * purl across, knit back plain, repeat from * until 57 rows are done, counting each time across as a row.

In knitting the heel, the *first* stitch in each row, whether it be a knitted or a purled row, should be slipped.

Now commence to decrease as follows, viz. : 58th row, k 13, s and b, k 10, n, k 3, s and b, k 10, n, k 13.——59th row, purl——60th row, k 13, s and b, k

8, n, k 3, s and b, k 8, n, k 13.——**61st row**, purl.——**62d row**, k 13, s and b, k 6, n, k 3, s and b, k 6, n, k 13.——**63d row**, purl.——**64th row**, k 13, s and b, k 4, n, k 3, s and b, k 4, n, k 13.——**65th row**, purl.——**66th row**, k 13, s and b, k 2, n, k 3, s and b, k 2, n, k 13.——**67th row**, purl.——**68th row**, k 13, s and b, n, k 3, s and b, n, k 13.——**69th row**, purl.——**70th row**, commence by k 17, ***, then fold needles together with wrong side of heel out, slip off the first stitch, **knit 2** together, taking one from each needle, pass slipped **stitch over**, and continue knitting 2 together and passing the last made stitch over **until all are dis-** posed of but one, which completes heel, which may now **be** turned right **side out.** Pick up and knit 1 stitch in each loop on **the side of** heel going towards left, **knit** across instep needle; pick up and knit in **the** loops on the opposite side **of** heel, 1 stitch in each as before, which completes first round in foot.

In knitting the second **round, extra** stitches must **be** made, one in every four on the sides of the heel only (not on instep), and in this round it is necessary **also** to decrease 2 by narrowing at right-hand corner, and s and b at left-hand corner **next** to instep. In **the** next 2 rounds decrease 2 in the same manner, and afterwards **de-** crease 2 in every alternate round until the whole number of stitches is reduced **to** 112, then continue knitting until the required length of foot is obtained. To decrease for toe, take an equal number of stitches **on each** needle, commence middle **of** instep needle, knit all but 3, **s and b**, k 1, on **next needle,** k 1, n, k until 3 are left, **s and b,** **k 1,** on **next** needle, k 1, n, k until 3 are left, **s and b,** k 1, at first corner **of** instep needle, **k** 1, n, k to middle of needle, which completes **first** round of decreasing for toe. **Knit** plain 3 rounds, then decrease in next round as **before. Knit** 3 rounds plain and decrease in next round **as** before. Knit 2 rounds **plain** and decrease in next **round as** before; knit 2 rounds plain and decrease in **next** round as before; knit 2 rounds plain and decrease in every round after, 1 stitch on each needle until **4** stitches are left **on** each needle; then knit 2 rounds plain and finish.

When decreasing only 1 stitch on **a needle** for toe, care must be taken **to** narrow at first corner of needles in the first round and s and b at the last corner in the next round, and so on alternately until done.

This rule will produce socks suitable **for a** man of **full size, and** the number of stitches should be less for a very small **foot or** for boys.

This rule for toe is suitable for all sizes of stockings, and a good heel for any size can be made by knitting and purling as many times across as there are stitches on the heel needle, before commencing to decrease.

The rule for decreasing in the heel will need **to be slightly changed in different sizes,** and any knitter on reading these directions **will** easily **see what changes are** required. The general rule for the number of stitches in **a heel is to take** one-half of the whole number in the ankle, and the number **should** be odd.

On completion it will improve the appearance of **the socks to lay a dry cloth over** them and press with a hot iron.

———

RULE F.

GENTS' SILK SOCKS.

Materials: **2 ounces** FLORENCE Knitting **Silk No. 500, and** four No. **22** knitting needles.

Cast 140 stitches on three needles, knit around once plain, then knit in ribs, alter- nating 4 stitches plain and 2 purl, until leg is 3½ inches long, then knit plain 6 inches, and commence heel by taking 71 stitches on one needle, * purl across, and knit back plain, repeat from * until 71 rows are done, counting each time across as a row.

In knitting the heel, the *first* stitch in each row, whether it be a knitted or a purled row, should be slipped.

Now commence to decrease as follows, viz.: **72d row**, k 16, s and b, k 14, n, k 3, s and b, k 14, n, k 16.——**73d row**, purl.——**74th row**, k 16, s and b, **k 12**, n, k 3, s and b, k 12, n, k 16.——**75th row**, purl.——**76th row, k 16, s and b**, k 10, n, k 3, s and b, k 10, n, **k 16.**——**77th row**, purl.——**78th row, k 16, s** and b, k 8, n, k 3, s and b, k 8, n, k 16.——**79th row**, purl.——**80th row**, k 16, s and b, k 6, n, k 3, s and b, k 6, n, k 16.——**81st row**, purl.——**82d row, k 16, s** and b, k 4, n, k 3, s and b, k 4, n, k 16.——**83d row**, purl.——**84th row, k 16**, s and b, k 2, n, k 3, s and b, k 2, n, k 16.——**85th row**, purl.——**86th row**, k 16, s and b, n, k 3, s and b, n, k 16.——**87th row**, purl.——**88th row**, commence by k 20. After this, proceed as in Rule E, for Gents' Silk Socks, from point marked ***, with this exception: instead of decreasing in the foot at instep to 112 stitches, decrease only until the number of stitches is reduced to 140.

RULE G.

LADIES' SILK STOCKINGS.

Materials: 4 ounces No. 300 **FLORENCE Knitting Silk**, and four No. 19 knitting needles.

Cast 160 stitches on three needles, knit around once plain, then knit in ribs, alternating 4 stitches plain and 2 purl 10 rounds, then knit plain (purling one stitch in each round in the middle of one needle, which forms the seam), until the leg is 12 inches long; then decrease† one stitch each side of seam in every third round until the whole number of stitches is reduced to 113, then knit 4½ inches and commence heel, by taking 28 stitches each side of seam, on one needle making 57 in all;* purl across (*knit* the seam stitch in this row), and knit back plain; (*purl* the seam stitch in this row) then repeat from * until 57 rows are done, counting each time across as a row.

In knitting the heel, the *first* stitch in each row, whether it be a **knitted or a purled** row, should be slipped.

Now commence to decrease as follows, viz.: **58th row**, k 13, s and b, k 10, n, k 1, p 1, k 1, s and b, k 10, n, k 13.——**59th row**, p 26, k 1, p 26.——**60th row**, k 13, s and b, k 8, n, k 1, p 1, k 1, s and b, k 8, n, k 13.——**61st row**, p 24, k 1, p 24.——**62d row**, k 13, s and b, k 6, n, k 1, p 1, k 1, s and b, k 6, n, k 13.——**63d row**, p 22, k 1, p 22.——**64th row**, k 13, s and b, k 4, n, k 1, p 1, k 1, s and b, k 4, n, k 13.——**65th row**, p 20, k 1, p 20.——**66th row**, k 13, s and b, k 2, n, k 1, p 1, k 1, s and b, k 2, n, k 13.——**67th row**, p 18, k 1, p 18.——**68th row**, k 13, s and b, n, k 1, p 1, k 1, s and b, n, k 13.——**69th row**, p 16, k 1, p 16.——**70th row**, commence by k 17, after this proceed as in Rule E, for Gents' Silk Socks, from point marked ***.

---

† The manner of decreasing each side of seam (referred to before) is as follows, viz.: Commence on the seam needle and knit all but 3 stitches on the right of the seam, then s and b and k 1; now purl the seam stitch, then k 1 and n, which completes operation of decreasing for one round.

RULE H.

LADIES' SILK STOCKINGS.

Materials : 3½ ounces No. 500 FLORENCE Knitting Silk, and four No. 22 knitting needles.

Cast 210 stitches on three needles, knit around once plain, then knit in ribs, alternating 4 stitches plain and 2 purl, 12 rounds, then knit plain (*purling one* stitch in each round in the middle of one needle, which forms the seam), until the leg is 12 inches long; then decrease† 1 stitch each side of seam in every 4th round, until the whole number of stitches is reduced to 140, then knit 4½ inches, and commence heel by taking 35 stitches each side of seam, on one needle, making 71 in all *; purl across (*knit* the seam stitch in this row); knit back plain (*purl* the seam stitch in this row), then repeat from * until 71 rows are done, counting each time across as a row.

In knitting the heel, the *first* stitch in each row, whether it be a knitted or a purled row, should be slipped.

Now commence to decrease as follows, viz.: 72d row, k 16, s and b, k 14, n, k 1, p 1, k 1, s and b, k 14, n, k 16. —— 73d row, p 33, k 1, p 33. —— 74th row, k 16, s and b, k 12, n, k 1, p 1, k 1, s and b, k 12, n, k 16. —— 75th row, p 31, k 1, p 31. —— 76th row, k 16, s and b, k 10, n, k 1, p 1, k 1, s and b, k 10, n, k 16. —— 77th row, k 29, k 1, p 29. —— 78th row, k 16, s and b, k 8, n, k 1, p 1, k 1, s and b, k 8, n, k 16. —— 79th row, p 27, k 1, p 27. —— 80th row, k 16, s and b, k 6, n, k 1, p 1, k 1, s and b, k 6, n, k 16. —— 81st row, p 25, k 1, p 25. —— 82d row, k 16, s and b, k 4, n, k 1, p 1, k 1, s and b, k 4, n, k 16. —— 83d row, p 23, k 1, p 23. —— 84th row, k 16, s and b, k 2, n, k 1, p 1, k 1, s and b, k 2, n, k 16. —— 85th row, p 21, k 1, p 21. —— 86th row, k 16, s and b, n, k 1, p 1, k 1, s and b, n, k 16. —— 87th row, p 19, k 1, p 19. —— 88th row, commence by k 20, after this proceed as in Rule E, for Gents' Silk Socks, from point marked ***, with this exception : instead of decreasing in the foot at instep to 112 stitches, decrease only until the number of stitches is reduced to 140.

RULE I.

Another Rule for knitting the Toe of a Stocking from Florence Knitting Silk.

The method of knitting the toe, in the foregoing rules, will produce stockings resembling the best French woven goods, but as some may prefer a different style, we give the following, which is also very good for finishing off a mitten in the hand:

Commence at corner of instep needle. ‡1st round, k 7, n, repeat until the number of stitches on all the needles is reduced so as to be divisible by nine, and knit balance of round plain. —— 2d round, knit plain. —— 3d round, k 7, n, repeat, and knit 7 rounds plain. —— 11th round, k 6, n, repeat, and knit 6 rounds plain. —— 18th round, k 5, n, repeat, and knit 5 rounds plain. —— 24th round, k 4, n, repeat, and knit 4 rounds plain. Now narrow once on each needle in every round until only 4 stitches are left on each needle, then narrow twice on each needle, and cast off. When decreasing once on each needle only, do not narrow at the same point in every round, but at a different place in each successive round.

---

† The manner of decreasing each side of seam (referred to before) is as follows, viz.: Commence on the seam needle, and knit all but 3 stitches on the right of the seam, then s and b and k 1; now purl the seam stitch, then k 1 and n, which completes operation of decreasing for one round.

‡ In case the number of stitches on the needles is already divisible by nine, then the 1st and 2d rounds should be omitted, commencing at once with the 3d round instead of the 1st.

Table showing Number of Stitches required for Stockings of various sizes (Children's, Misses, and Ladies') with No. 19 Needles, and No. 300 Florence Knitting Silk.

	5 In. Foot.	5½ In. Foot.	6 In. Foot.	6½ In. Foot.	7 In. Foot.	7½ In. Foot.	8 In. Foot.	8½ In. Foot.	9 In. Foot.	9½ In. Foot.
Number of stitches needed for top of stocking,	108	112	116	124	132	140	148	156	162	169
Number of rounds before beginning to decrease* for ankle, including 20 rounds ribbed,	140	150	160	185	190	200	210	220	230	240
Whole number of rounds before commencing heel,	250	265	295	340	355	370	380	390	400	410
Number of stitches in ankle, after decreasing,*	78	82	86	90	94	98	102	106	110	113
Number of stitches in heel, including centre or seam stitch,	39	41	43	45	47	49	51	53	55	57
Number of rows in heel, before decrease,† counting each time across,	39	41	43	45	47	49	51	53	55	57
Amount of silk required for one pair of stockings,	2 oz.	2 oz.	2½ oz.	2½ oz.	3 oz.	3 oz.	3½ oz.	3½ oz.	4 oz.	4 oz.
Length of toe, from commencement of decrease to point,	$1\frac{10}{20}$ in.	$1\frac{11}{20}$ in.	$1\frac{12}{20}$ in.	$1\frac{13}{20}$ in.	$1\frac{14}{20}$ in.	$1\frac{15}{20}$ in.	$1\frac{16}{20}$ in.	$1\frac{17}{20}$ in.	$1\frac{18}{20}$ in.	$1\frac{19}{20}$ in.
Length of foot, before commencing to decrease for toe, including width of heel at widest point,	$3\frac{12}{20}$ in.	$3\frac{12}{20}$ in.	$4\frac{8}{20}$ in.	$4\frac{17}{20}$ in.	$5\frac{6}{20}$ in.	$5\frac{15}{20}$ in.	$6\frac{4}{20}$ in.	$6\frac{13}{20}$ in.	$7\frac{2}{20}$ in.	$7\frac{11}{20}$ in.

* For manner of decreasing in leg, also in foot, see Rule G.
† For manner of decreasing for bottom of heel, see page 34. The number of stitches in the foot, after decreasing for instep, should be the same as in the ankle.

Table showing Number of Stitches required for Stockings of various sizes (Children's, Misses' and Ladies') with No. 22 Needles, and No. 500 Florence Knitting Silk.

	5 In. Foot.	5½ In. Foot.	6 In. Foot.	6½ In. Foot.	7 In. Foot.	7½ In. Foot.	8 In. Foot.	8½ In. Foot.	9 In. Foot.	9½ In. Foot.
Number of stitches needed for top of stocking,	135	140	145	155	165	175	185	195	202	210
Number of rounds before beginning to decrease* for ankle, including 24 rounds ribbed,	168	180	192	222	228	240	252	264	276	288
Whole number of rounds before commencing heel,	300	318	354	408	426	444	456	468	480	492
Number of stitches in ankle, after decreasing,*	98	102	108	113	118	122	127	132	137	142
Number of stitches in heel, including centre or seam stitch,	49	51	55	57	59	61	63	67	69	71
Number of rows in heel, before decreasing,† counting each time across,	49	51	55	57	59	61	63	67	69	71
Amount of silk required for one pair of stockings,	1¼ oz.	1½ oz.	2 oz.	2¼ oz.	2½ oz.	3 oz.	3 oz.	3 oz.	3½ oz.	3½ oz.
Length of toe, from commencement of decrease to point,	$1\frac{10}{20}$ in.	$1\frac{11}{20}$ in.	$1\frac{12}{20}$ in.	$1\frac{13}{20}$ in.	$1\frac{14}{20}$ in.	$1\frac{15}{20}$ in.	$1\frac{16}{20}$ in.	$1\frac{17}{20}$ in.	$1\frac{18}{20}$ in.	$1\frac{19}{20}$ in.
Length of foot, before commencing to decrease for toe, including width of heel at widest point,	$3\frac{12}{20}$ in.	$3\frac{16}{20}$ in.	$4\frac{8}{20}$ in.	$4\frac{17}{20}$ in.	$5\frac{6}{20}$ in.	$5\frac{15}{20}$ in.	$6\frac{4}{20}$ in.	$6\frac{13}{20}$ in.	$7\frac{6}{20}$ in.	$7\frac{15}{20}$ in.

* For manner of decreasing in leg, also in foot, see Rule II.
† For manner of decreasing for bottom of heel see page 34. The number of stitches in the foot, after decreasing for instep, should be the same as in the ankle.

† Decreasing in the heel is done at four points in every row where plain knitting is done, no decrease being made in the purled rows.

The number of stitches in a heel should always be odd, the central or seam stitch dividing the whole number into two sections, each containing an even number of stitches.

The decreasing should be done at two points in each section, once next the seam, and again at a point about one-half way between this decrease and the edge of the heel on either side the seam, thus disposing of 4 stitches in each decreased row. The first stitch on either side of the seam should be knit plain in every decreased row.

The manner of decreasing is shown in Rules G and H, and to further illustrate the principle which should govern the work in hand, the details are given below for completing the heel of the child's stocking with 5 inch foot. (See table, page 33).

The number of stitches in this heel is 39. After completing 39 rows, decrease as follows, viz.: 40th row, k 8, s and b, k 6, n, k 1, p 1, k 1, s and b, k 6, n, k 8. ——41st row, p 17, k 1, p 17.——42d row, k 8, s and b, k 4, n, k 1, p 1, k 1, s and b, k 4, n, k 8.——43d row, p 15, k 1, p 15.——44th row, k 8, s and b, k 2, n, k 1, p 1, k 1, s and b, k 2, n, k 8.——45th row, p 13, k 1, p 13.——46th row, k 8, s and b, n, k 1, p 1, k 1, s and b, n, k 8.——47th row, p 11, k 1, p 11.—— 48th row, commence by k 12, after this proceed as in Rule E for gents' silk socks, from point marked ***. The number of stitches on the needles will be much less than in Rule E, however, and that number will be decreased to shape the instep until only 78 stitches remain.

It will be observed that the number of stitches in the heel *between* the two points of decrease, diminishes by two in each section or four in each decreased row, until none are left, the two points of decrease coming in contact. This forms, when the heel is complete, "gores" which come together on both sides the heel at the bottom like letter V. Thus it will be seen that whenever the point of the V-shaped figure is reached, no further decrease is needed, and the next step is to purl back one row, and commence the following row by knitting one-half the number of stitches and one more, then fold needles and cast off as described in Rule E.

RULE 25.

BABY'S SOCK, WITH IMITATION SLIPPER. (Fig. 25.)

Materials: ½ oz. pink and ½ oz. white No. 300 FLORENCE Knitting Silk, and four No. 18 knitting needles.

With the pink silk, cast on to each of three needles 24 stitches, making 72 stitches; purl 3 rounds, and knit 3 rounds plain.

Commence the open-work pattern (which is in twelves, and is repeated six times in each round), and knit as follows with the white silk, viz.: 7th round, n, n, tto, k 1, tto, k 2, tto, k 1, tto, n, n, repeat.——8th and 9th rounds, plain. —— Repeat these three rounds until you have done 56 rounds of the white open-work —— Knit all of the 57th round plain, transfer the last stitch from the third needle to the first needle, and 13 stitches from the second needle to the first needle.

Having 38 stitches on the first needle, commence knitting in rows, instead of rounds, for the instep (leaving the heel until later), as follows, viz.: 1st row, s 1, * n, n, tto, k 1, tto, k 2, tto, k 1, tto, n, n, repeat from *, end with k 1.—— 2d row, s 1, purl 37.——3d row, s 1, k 37. —— 4th row, s 1, * p 2 together,

FLORENCE KNITTING SILK.   35

p 2 together, tto, p 1, tto, p 2, tto, p 1, tto, p 2 together, p 2 together, repeat from *, end with p 1.——5th row, s 1, k 37.——6th row, s 1, p 37. Repeat from the 1st row to the 6th row inclusive, until you have done 30 rows, all with the white silk.

Leave the first needle in the instep, and with pink silk cast on to your fourth needle 14 stitches extra (these are for one of the straps to the slippers); knit with same needle the 34 stitches from the second and third needles in the order named, and cast on 14 more new stitches for the other strap to slipper. You have now 62 stitches for heel and straps, which work in rows.

1st row, knit plain.——2d, 3d, 5th, and 6th rows, purl.—— 4th row, k 2, tto, n, repeat until 2 stitches remain, which knit.——7th row, knit plain. —— 8th row, cast off 14 stitches, k 48. —— 9th row, cast off 14 stitches, p 34.—— 10th, 11th, 14th, 17th, 18th, 20th, 21st, 24th, 27th, 28th, 30th, 31st, 34th and 37th rows, s 1, k 33.——12th, 13th, 15th, 16th, 19th, 22d, 23d, 25th, 26th, 29th, 32d, 33d, 35th and 36th rows, s 1, p 33.——38th row, s 1, k 22, s and h, turn.——39th and every alternate row, up to and including the 57th, s 1, p 12, p 2 together, turn. —— 40th and every alternate row, up to and including the 56th, s 1, k 12, s and h, turn.—— Next pick up on the left side of heel 16 loops and purl the same as part of the 57th row. Turn, k 30, and pick up on the other side of heel 16 more loops and knit as part of 58th row,——59th row, k 16, p 14, k 14, n.——60th row, p 15, k 14, p 14, p 2 together.——61st row, p 42, p 2 together.——62d row, k 41, n.——63d row, p 40, p 2 together.——64th row, p 13, k 14, p 12, p 2 together.——65th row, k 13, p 14, k 11, n.——66th row, k 37, n.——67th row, p 36, p 2 together.——68th row, k 35, n.——69th row, k 11, p 14, k 9, n.——70th row, p 10, k 14, p 9, p 2 together.——71st row, p 32, p 2 together.——72d row, k 31, n.——73d row, p 30, p 2 together.——74th row, p 8, k 14, p 7, p 2 together.——75th row, k 8, p 14, k 6, n.——76th row, k 27, n.——77th row, p 26, p 2 together.——78th row, k 25, n.——79th row, k 6, p 14, k 4, n.——80th row, p 5, k 14, p 4, p 2 together.——81st row, p 24.——82d row, k 24.——83d row, p 24.——84th row, p 5, k 14, p 5.——85th row, k 5, p 14, k 5.——86th row, k 24.——87th row, p 24.——88th row, k 24. —— 89th row, k 5, p 14, k 5.——90th row, p 5, k 14, p 5.——91st row, p 24.——92d row, k 24. —— 93d row, p 24.

Now commence working in rounds with four needles, but first rearrange the stitches, by placing those which are on the instep needle on two needles (19 on each).

Hereafter we shall speak of those needles as the second and third, and the other needle, which now holds the stitches forming the bottom and sides of the sock, as the first.

Transfer 5 stitches from the first to the third needle and 5 more from the first to the second needle. Having 14 stitches on the first and 24 on each of the other needles, knit plain the 5 stitches remaining undisposed of on the third needle.

Hereafter the stitches on the first needle are all knit plain in every round, and those on the other needles are worked alternately 2 rounds purled, and 3 rounds knit plain.

The first decrease for toe is in the 2d round of purling, and occurs in this and in every alternate round thereafter, at the first corner of the second and the last corner of the third needles, either by narrowing or purling, as the case may be, until 23 stitches only remain on three needles, then decrease twice at each of said corners in each of the next 2 rounds.

Transfer the stitches from the second to the third needle, and knit the 10 stitches on this needle with the 10 on the first needle *together*, casting off as you knit.

Finish the sock by twisting a cord from the pink silk, and running the same into the open work of the ankle and straps, tipping with tassels of the same color.

—

RULE 26.

BABY'S SOCK.　(Fig. 26.)

Materials: ¼ ounce pink and ¼ ounce white No. 300 FLORENCE Knitting Silk and four No. 18 knitting needles.

FIG. 26.

With the pink silk, cast on to the first needle 27 stitches, to the second needle 18 stitches, and to the third needle 27 stitches, making 72 in all, and knit 5 rounds plain. **6th round,** n, tto, repeat —— Knit 5 rounds plain. ——**12th round,** pick up, and knit with each stitch on the needles, one loop from the edge where your work was commenced, thus forming a hem for the sock. The loops should be picked up from the back side of the work.——**13th round,** with white. s and b, k 2, tto, k 1, tto, k 2, n, repeat. ——**14th round,** with white, knit plain. —— **15th round,** with white, s and b, k 1, tto, k 3, tto, k 1, n, repeat —— **16th round,** with white, knit plain. Repeat the last four rounds, alternating pink with white silk with each repetition until you have nine white and eight pink shells, the last repetition being with white.

Commence the next round with pink, knitting 24 stitches. Transfer the remaining 3 stitches to the second needle. Transfer 15 stitches from the third needle to the first needle, making 30 stitches on the first needle, which are to constitute the foundation of the heel. The remaining 33 stitches, which are to form the instep, will be left undisturbed on the second and third needles until the heel is finished. Then, with pink, purl back on the first needle one row.

Work 34 rows on the first needle, as follows, viz.: s 1, k 38. —— 36th row, s 1, k 24, n, turn. Work 25 rows as follows, viz.: s 1, k 11, n, turn. Knit one row plain, and form on same needle 19 stitches from the loops on the left-hand side of heel. Transfer 3 stitches from the second needle to the first, and knit the same. Transfer all the stitches but 3 on the third needle to the second needle. You now have 27 stitches on the second needle. With these stitches, s and b, k 2, tto, k 1, tto, k 2, n, s and b, k 2, tto, k 1, tto, k 2, n, s and b, k 2, tto, k 1, tto, k 2, tto, n. Knit the 3 stitches on the third needle, and form 19 stitches from the loops on the right-hand side of heel. Transfer 6 stitches from the first needle to the third and knit the same. This completes the **1st round** of the foot. **2d round**, with pink, n, k 23, n, k 31, s and b, k 24. —— **3d round**, k 27, s and b, k 1, tto, k 3, tto, k 1, n, s and b, k 1, tto, k 3, tto, k 1, n, s and b, k 1, tto, k 3, tto, k 1, n, k 27. —— **4th round**, k 23, n, k 31, s and b, k 23.

This completes the first pink stripe in the foot, there being four pink and four white in all, each of which **requires** 4 rounds to complete. The 27 stitches on the second, or instep needle, are **to be** knit as three repetitions of the fancy pattern described in the **13th, 14th, 15th** and **16th rounds** of this rule until the eight stripes are complete.

Decrease on the first and third needles, once on each, in every alternate round until the number of stitches on each of these needles is reduced to eighteen.

The manner of decreasing on first needle, is to knit all but four stitches, n, k 2. The manner of decreasing on third needle, is to k 2, s and b, knit the remaining stitches.

Having completed the eight stripes, the fancy open-work is discontinued, and the toe, which is knit from pink, is worked as follows, viz.: 1st, 3d, 5th, 7th, 9th, 11th and 13th rounds, knit plain. —— **2d, 4th, 6th, 8th, 10th, 12th** and **14th** rounds, purl. —— 15th **round, knit plain,** narrowing twice on each needle. —— 16th round, purl. —— **17th round, knit plain.** —— 18th round, purl. —— 19th round, knit plain, narrowing twice on each needle. —— **20th** round, purl. —— 21st round, knit plain. —— **22d** round, purl. —— **23d round,** knit plain, narrowing twice on each needle. —— **24th round,** purl. —— **25th** round, knit plain. —— 26th **round,** purl, decreasing once on each needle. —— 27th round, **knit plain.** —— **28th round,** purl. —— **29th round,** knit plain, narrowing once on each needle. —— **30th round,** purl. Commence the 31st round by knitting 10 stitches. Transfer 10 stitches from third needle to first, thus placing 20 stitches on each of two needles. Cast off, knitting together at same time one stitch from each needle.

Finish the sock by twisting a cord from the pink and white silk, and running the same into a row of the open-work of the ankle, tipping with tassels of the same color.

If but one color is used, one-half ounce of silk will suffice for a pair of socks.

RULE 27.

BABY'S SOCK. (Fig. 27.)

Materials: ½ ounce light blue and ½ ounce cream white No. 300 FLORENCE Knitting Silk, and four No. 18 knitting needles.

With the blue silk, cast on to the first needle 28 stitches, and on to each of the second and third needles 21 stitches, making 70 in all, and knit 5 rounds plain.

6th round, n, tto, repeat.——Knit 5 rounds plain.——12th round, pick up and knit with each stitch on the needles, one loop from the edge where your work was commenced, thus forming a hem for the sock. The loops should be picked up from the back side of the work.——13th round, with white, knit plain.——14th round, with white, p 3, k 1, p 3, repeat.——15th round, with blue, knit plain.——16th round, with blue, s and b, k 1, tto, k 1, tto, k 1, n, repeat.——17th round, with white, knit plain.——18th round, with white, p 3, k 1, p 3, repeat. —— Repeat the last four rounds, alternating blue with white silk with each repetition until you have formed seventeen of the white ribs, which will require 68 rounds. Transfer 7 stitches from the first needle to the second, 14 stitches from the second needle to the third, and 21 stitches from the third needle to the first, making 42 stitches on the first needle, which are to constitute the foundation of the heel. The

FIG. 27.

remaining 28 stitches which are to form the instep, will be left undisturbed on the second and third needles until the heel is finished.

Knit 21 stitches, turn.——1st row, s 1, k 20, p 21, turn.——Work 34 rows as follows, viz.: s 1, k 41.——36th row, s 1, k 26, n, turn.——Work 27 rows as follows, viz.: s 1, k 12, n, turn. Knit one row plain, and form 17 stitches from the loops on the left-hand side of heel. Knit the stitches on second and third needles on to one needle, which call the second or instep needle, and on the third needle form 17 stitches from the loops on the right-hand side of heel. Transfer 7 stitches from the first to the third needle and knit the same. Transfer 3 stitches from the second needle to the first and 3 stitches from the second needle to the third. This completes the 1st round of the foot. ——2d round, with blue, k 23, n, k 3, tto, k 1, n, s and b, k 1, tto, k 1, tto, k 1, n, s and b, k 1, tto, k 1, tto, k 1, n, s and b, k 1, tto, k 3, s and b, k 23. This completes the first blue open-work stripe in the foot. Work alternately with blue and white two rounds of each, until you have twelve stripes of each color.

The fancy open-work pattern in instep is knit on the 22 stitches on the second needle as follows, viz.: 1st round, with white, (second needle) knit plain.—— 2d round, with white, k 1, p 6, k 1, p 6, k 1, p 6, k 1.——3d round, with blue, knit plain.——4th round, with blue, k 1, tto, k 1, n, s and b, k 1, tto, k 1, tto, k 1, n, s and b, k 1, tto, k 1, tto, k 1, n, s and b, k 1, tto, k 1. Repeat these 4 rounds until the requisite number of stripes is obtained. On the first and third needles, while work on the fancy pattern in instep is progressing, the two colors of silk are used, alternating 2 rounds of each as in the instep, first knitting plain with white one round, and purling with white one round. Knit the next 2 rounds plain with blue.

Decrease on the first and third needles, once on each, in every alternate round, until the number of stitches on each needle is reduced to twenty-one.

The manner of decreasing on first needle is to knit or purl all but four stitches, n, k 2. The manner of decreasing on third needle is to k 2, s and h, knit the remaining stitches. After the twelfth white stripe in foot is complete, knit the toe with blue as follows, viz.: 1st and 2d rounds, knit plain.——3d round, knit plain, narrowing twice on each needle.——4th round, purl.——5th round, knit plain.——6th round, purl.——7th round, knit plain, narrowing twice on each needle.——8th round, purl.——9th round, knit plain.——10th round, purl.——11th round, knit plain, narrowing twice on each needle.——12th round, purl.——13th round, knit plain.——14th round, purl, decreasing once on each needle.——15th round, knit plain.——16th round, purl.——17th round, knit plain, narrowing once on each needle.——18th round, purl. Transfer 1 stitch from the first needle to the second, and 1 stitch from the third needle to the second.

Commence the **19th round** by knitting 12 stitches. Transfer 12 stitches from third needle to first, thus placing 24 stitches on each of two needles. Cast off, knitting together at same time one stitch from each needle.

Finish the sock by twisting a cord from the blue and white silk, and running the same into a row of the open-work of the ankle, tipping with tassels of the same color.

If but one color is used, one-half ounce of silk will be enough for a pair of socks.

RULE 28.

FANCY PATTERN. (Fig. 28.)

This design is in tens, is knit on four needles, and is complete in 2 rounds. Having cast on any number of stitches divisible by ten, and knit 1 round plain, knit the pattern as follows, viz.: 1st round, k 1, tto, k 3, s 1, n, pass s over, k 3, tto, repeat.——2d round, knit plain.

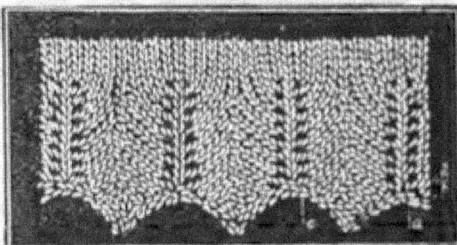

FIG. 28.

RULE 29.

FANCY PATTERN. (Fig. 29.)

This design is in nines, is knit on four needles, and is complete in 8 rounds. 1st round, k 3, n, tto, k 4, repeat.——2d, 4th, 6th and 8th rounds, knit plain.——3d round, k 2, n, tto, n, tto, k 3, repeat.——5th round, k 1, n, tto, n, tto, n, tto, k 2, repeat.——7th round, n, tto, n, tto, n, tto, n, tto, k 1, repeat.

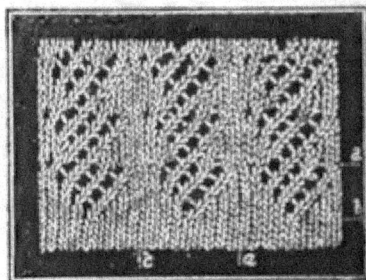

FIG. 29.

RULE 30.

FANCY PATTERN. (Fig. 30.)

This design is in nines, is knit on four needles, and is complete in 12 rounds.

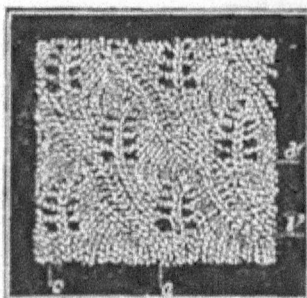

FIG. 30.

1st round, s and b, k 5, tto, k 1, tto, k 1, repeat. —— 2d round, s and b, k 8, repeat —— 4th, 6th, 8th, 10th and 12th rounds, same as 2d. —— 3d round, s and b, k 4, tto, k 1, tto, k 2, repeat. —— 5th round, s and b, k 3, tto, k 1, tto, k 3, repeat. —— 7th round, s and b, k 2, tto, k 1, tto, k 4, repeat —— 9th round, s and b, k 1, tto, k 1, tto, k 5, repeat. —— 11th round, s and b, tto, k 1, tto, k 6, repeat.

NOTE.—In the 2d, 4th, 6th, 8th, 10th and 12th rounds you have 10 stitches on the needles in each pattern instead of 9, as in other rounds.

RULE 31.

FANCY PATTERN. (Fig. 31.)

This design is in fourteens, is knit on four needles, and is complete in 12 rounds.

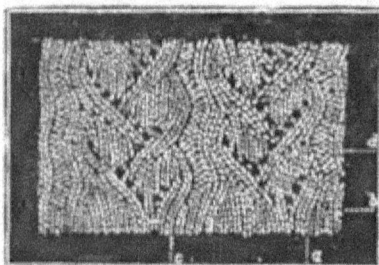

FIG. 31.

1st round, k 2, tto, k 1, tto, k 1, s and b, k 3, n, k 1, p 2, repeat. —— 2d and every alternate round, including 12th, k 12, p 2, repeat. —— 3d round, k 2, tto, k 3, tto, k 1, s and b, k 1, n, k 1, p 2, repeat. —— 5th round, k 2, tto, k 5, tto, k 1, s 1, n, pass s over, k 1, p 2, repeat. —— 7th round, s and b, k 3, n, k 1, tto, k 1, tto, k 3, p 2, repeat. —— 9th round, s and b, k 1, n, k 1, tto, k 3, tto, k 3, p 2, repeat. —— 11th round, s 1, n, pass s over, k 1, tto, k 5, tto, k 3, p 2, repeat.

RULE 32.

FANCY PATTERN. (Fig. 32.)

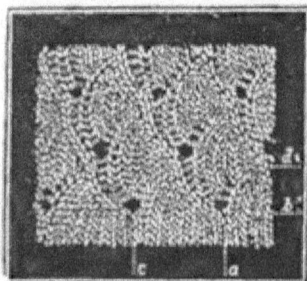

FIG. 32.

This design is in eights, is knit on four needles, and is complete in 7 rounds. 1st round, s and b, k 6, tto, repeat. —— 2d round, s and b, k 5, tto, k 1, repeat. —— 3d round, s and b, k 4, tto, k 2, repeat. —— 4th round, s and b, k 3, tto, k 3, repeat —— 5th round, s and b, k 2, tto, k 4, repeat. —— 6th round, s and b, k 1, tto, k 5, repeat. —— 7th round, s and b, tto, k 6, repeat.

RULE 33.

FANCY PATTERN. (Fig. 33.)

The design is in sixes, is knit on four needles, and is complete in 12 rounds.

1st round, k 2, n, tto, k 2.——2d and every alternate round, including 12th, knit plain.—— 3d round, k 1, n, tto, k 3, repeat.——5th round, n, tto, k 4, repeat. After knitting plain all of the 6th round, *except the last stitch*, transfer the last stitch on each needle to the next needle. 7th round, n, tto, k 1, tto, s and b, k 1, repeat.——9th round, k 4, tto, s and b, repeat. After knitting the 10th round, which is plain, transfer the first stitch on each needle to the next needle, thereby leaving 1 stitch on the third needle to be considered as part of the 10th round, and knit as such in addition to the sixes already disposed of. 11th round, k 1, n, tto, k 1, tto, s and b, repeat. To repeat the pattern, begin with the 5th round and end with the 12th.

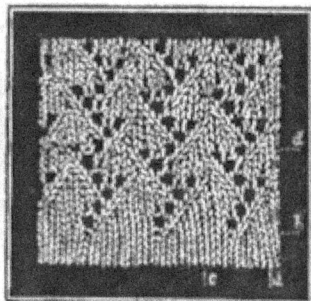

FIG. 33.

RULE 34.

FANCY PATTERN. (Fig. 34.)

This design is in fours, is knit on four needles, and is complete in 12 rounds. 1st round, k 2, n, tto, repeat.——2d and every alternate round, including the 12th, knit plain. ——3d round, k 1, n, tto, k 1, repeat.——5th round, n, tto, k 2, repeat.——7th round, k 2, tto, s and b, repeat. After knitting the 8th round, which is plain, transfer the first stitch on each needle to the next needle, thereby leaving 1 stitch on the third needle to be considered as part of the 8th round, and knit as such in addition to the fours already disposed of.——9th round, k 2, tto, s and b, repeat.——11th round, n, tto, k 2, repeat. After knitting plain all of the 12th round, *except the last stitch*, transfer the last stitch on each needle to the next needle. To repeat the pattern, begin with the 5th round and end with the 12th, including both transfers of stitches.

FIG. 34.

RULE 35.

FANCY PATTERN. (Fig. 35.)

This design is in sixes, is knit on four needles, and is complete in 14 rounds.

1st round, n, tto, n, tto, n, tto, repeat.—— 2d, 3d and 4th rounds, knit plain.—— 5th round, k 4, n, tto, repeat.——6th round, k 3, n, tto, k 1, repeat.——7th round, k 2, n, tto, k 2, repeat.——8th round, k 1, n, tto, k 3, repeat.——9th round, n, tto, k 4, repeat.—— 10th, 11th and 12th rounds, knit plain.—— 13th round, n, tto, n, tto, n, tto, repeat.—— 14th round, knit plain.

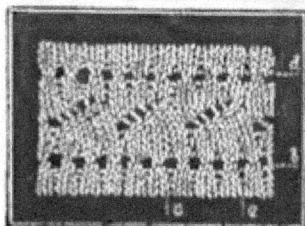

FIG. 35.

RULE 36.

FANCY PATTERN. (Fig. 36.)

This design is in sixes, is knit on four needles, and is complete in 16 rounds. 1st round, n, tto, n, tto, n, tto, repeat.—2d, 3d and 4th rounds, knit plain.—5th round, k 3, n, tto, k 1, repeat.—6th round, k 2, n, tto, k 2, repeat.—7th round, k 1, n, tto, k 3, repeat.—8th round, n, tto, k 4, repeat,—9th round, k 2, tto, s and b, k 2, repeat.—10th round, k 3, tto, s and b, k 1, repeat.—11th round, k 4, tto, s and b, repeat.—12th, 13th and 14th rounds, knit plain.—15th round, n, tto, n, tto, n, tto, repeat—16th round, knit plain.

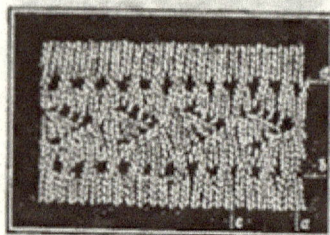

FIG. 36.

RULE 37.

FANCY PATTERN. (Fig. 37.)

This design is in sevens, is knit on four needles, and is complete in 11 rounds. 1st round, s and b, k 5, tto, repeat.—2d round, s and b, k 4, tto, k 1, repeat.—3d round, s and b, k 3, tto, k 2, repeat.—4th round, s and b, k 2, tto, k 3, repeat.—5th round, s and b, k 1, tto, k 4, repeat.—6th round, s and b, tto, k 5, repeat. Now transfer the first stitch on each needle to the next needle, thereby leaving 1 stitch on the third needle to be considered as part of the 6th round, and knit as such in addition to the sevens already disposed of. 7th round, k 1, tto, k 4, n, repeat.—8th round, k 2, tto, k 3, n, repeat—9th round, k 3, tto, k 2, n, repeat.—10th round, k 4, tto, k 1, n, repeat.—11th round, k 5, tto, n, repeat. Now transfer the last stitch on each needle to the next needle, and in *repeating* the pattern, *begin with the second round.*

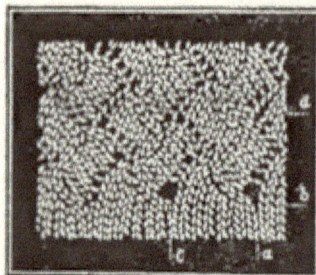

FIG. 37.

RULE 38.

FANCY PATTERN. (Fig. 38.)

This design is in sixes, is knit on four needles, and is complete in 20 rounds. 1st round, k 1, n, tto, k 3, repeat.—2d and every alternate round, including the 20th, knit plain.—3d round, n, tto, k 1, tto, s and b, k 1, repeat.—5th round, k 1, n, tto, k 3, repeat.—7th round, n, tto, k 1, tto, s and b, k 1, repeat. After knitting the 8th round, which is plain, transfer the first stitch on each needle to the next needle, thereby leaving one stitch on the third needle to be considered as part of the 8th round, and knit as such in addition to the sixes already disposed of.——9th round, tto, k 3, tto, s 1, n, pass s over, repeat.——11th round, tto, s and b,

FIG. 38.

k 1, n, tto, k 1, repeat.——13th round, k 1, tto, s 1, n, pass s over, tto, k 2, repeat. ——15th round, k 1, n, tto, k 3, repeat.——17th round, n, tto, k 1, tto, s and b, k 1, repeat.——19th round, k 1, n, tto, k 3, repeat.

RULE 39.

FANCY PATTERN. (Fig. 39.)

This design is in fourteens, is knit on four needles, and is complete in 14 rounds.

1st round, k 7, tto, k 5, n, repeat.——2d and 9th rounds, knit plain.——3d round, s and b, k 5, tto, k 1, tto, k 4, n, repeat.——4th round, s and b, k 4, tto, k 3, tto, k 3, n, repeat.——5th round, s and b, k 3, tto, k 5, tto, k 2, n, repeat.——6th round, s and b, k 2, tto, k 7, tto, k 1, n, repeat.——7th round, s and b, k 1, tto, k 9, tto, n, repeat.——8th round, s and b, k 5, tto, k 7, repeat.——10th round, s and b, k 4, tto, k 1, tto, k 5, n, repeat.——11th round, s and b, k 3, tto, k 3, tto, k 4,

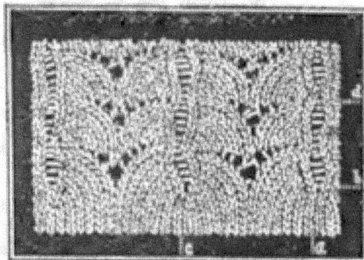

FIG. 39.

n, repeat.——12th round, s and b, k 2, tto, k 5, tto, k 3, n, repeat.——13th round, s and b, k 1, tto, k 7, tto, k 2, n, repeat.——14th round, s and b, tto, k 0, tto, k 1, n, repeat.

RULE 40.

FANCY PATTERN. (Fig. 40.)

This design is in sixes, is knit on four needles, and is complete in 8 rounds. 1st round, k 1, n, tto, k 3, repeat.——2d, 4th, 6th and 8th rounds, knit plain ——3d round, n, tto, k 1, tto, s and b, k 1. After knitting the 4th round, which is plain, transfer the first stitch on each needle to the next needle, thereby leaving 1 stitch on the third needle to be considered as part of the 4th round, and knit as such in addition to the sixes already disposed of. —— 5th round, tto, k 3, tto, s 1, n, pass s over, repeat.——7th round, tto, k 4, n, repeat.

FIG. 40.

RULE 41.

FANCY PATTERN. (Fig. 41.)

This design is in fours, is knit on four needles, and is complete in 4 rounds. 1st round, k 1, n, tto, k 1, repeat.——2d round, knit plain.——3d round, n, tto, k 2, repeat.——4th round, knit plain.

FIG. 41.

RULE 42.

LAMP SHADE. (Fig. 42.)

Materials: a piece of satin 7¼ inches wide and 29½ inches long, one ball of No. 300 FLORENCE Knitting Silk, and one spool Corticelli Sewing Silk; all of one color.

Sew the ends of the satin together, make a narrow hem on its lower edge, and turn down the upper edge 1½ inches in depth on the back side.

Shirr the top in 4 rows, placing the shirrings ¼ of an inch apart, with the 1st row ½ inch from the edge.

Draw up the satin in the 1st shirring so that the shade will be about 13 inches in circumference. Each successive shirring should be done so that the satin shall be a little wider than at the point of the previous row, so as to give a proper shape for the globe.

Lay a tape measure or yard-stick on the back side of the satin, and with a sharp lead-pencil mark small dots close to the narrow hem exactly ¼ of an inch apart. This insures uniform work in crocheting an edge for the fringe, which is to be made as follows, viz.: With a fine crochet-hook draw the end of the knitting silk through the satin exactly on the first dot previously marked by the pencil, put same over needle, make one chain, continue this operation on each dot entirely around the bottom of the shade and secure the ends. Then wind the knitting silk around a smooth, stiff piece of pasteboard 3¾ inches wide, say 50 times (but not so tight as to bend the board); cut the silk on one edge of the board, thus making 50 pieces of fringe 7½ inches long. As 600 of these pieces will be required, out that number in like manner, and with a coarse crotchet-hook draw 3, doubled as shown in Fig. 42, into each loop of the crotcheted edge. This forms a beautiful and durable fringe about 3¾ inches deep, which will not untwist *if made of* FLORENCE Knitting Silk, and completes a shade costing less than $1.00 for material, and requiring but little labor or skill.

FIG. 42.

If desired, the satin may be decorated either in Kensington work with FLORENCE Filling Silk, in outline designs with No. 1000 FLORENCE Etching Silk, or with painting.

Whether plain or decorated, these shades are very elegant, and will be found most acceptable wedding or holiday presents.

LACE EDGINGS AND INSERTIONS.

NOTE.—If the designs which follow are knit from No. 300 FLORENCE Knitting Silk on No. 16 needles, the laces will be twice as wide as shown in engraving.

RULE 43.

LACE EDGING. (Fig. 43.)

Cast on 13 stitches, knit across plain. **1st row,** s 1, k 1, tto twice, p 2 together, k 1, n, tto, k 1, tto, n, k 1, tto twice, k 2.——**2d row,** k 3, p 1, k 2, tto, k 3, tto, k 2, tto twice, p 2 together, k 2.——**3d row,** s 1, k 1, tto twice, p 2 together, k 2, tto, k 5, tto, n, k 4.——**4th row,** cast off 2, k 2, tto, k 3, tto, n, k 2, tto, k 2, tto twice, p 2 together, k 2.——**5th row,** s 1, k 1, tto twice, p 2 together, n, k 1, tto, n, k 3, n, tto, k 1, n, k 1.—— **6th row,** k 4, tto, n, k 1, n, tto, k 1, n, tto twice, p 2 together, k 2.——**7th row,** s 1, k 1, tto twice, p 2 together, n, k 1, tto twice, p 3 to-

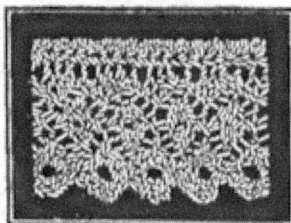

FIG. 43.

gether, tto, k 1, n, k 2.——**8th row,** k 9, tto twice, p 2 together, k 2. Repeat.

1 oz. silk No. 300 makes 2 yds. 35 inches above pattern.

1 oz. silk No. 500 makes 5 yds. 6 inches above pattern.

RULE 44.

LACE EDGING. (Fig. 44.)

Cast on 15 stitches, knit across plain. **1st row,** k 3, tto, n, k 3, tto, k 1, tto, k 6.—— **2d row,** k 6, tto, k 3, tto, n, k 3, tto, n, k 1.——**3d row,** k 3, tto, n, n, tto, k 5, tto, k 6 ——**4th row,** cast off 4, k 1, tto, n, k 3, n, tto, n, k 1, tto, n, k 1.——**5th row,** k 3, tto, n, k 1, tto, n, k 1, n, tto, k 3.—— **6th row,** k 3, tto, k 1, tto, s 2, k 1, pass the two slipped stitches over the knitted one, tto, k 4, tto, n, k 1. Repeat.

1 oz. silk No. 300 makes 2 yds. 35 inches above pattern.

1 oz. silk No. 500 makes 5 yds. 6 inches above pattern.

FIG. 44.

RULE 45.

LACE EDGING. (Fig. 45.)

Cast on 19 stitches, knit across plain. 1st row, s 1, k 1, tto, n, tto, n, p 2, k 1, tto, k 1, tto, k 1, p 2, k 2, tto twice, n, tto twice, k 2.——2d row, k 3, p 1, k 2, p1, k 4, p 5, k 2, p 5, k 1.——3d row, s 1, k 1, tto, n, tto, n, p 2, k 2, tto, k 1, tto, k 2, p 2, k 9.——4th row, k 11, p 7, k 2, p 5, k 1.——5th row, s 1, k 1, tto, n, tto, n, p 2, k 3, tto, k 1, tto, k 3, p 2, k 2, tto twice, n, tto twice, n, tto twice, n, k 1.——6th row, k 3, p 1, k 2, p 1, k 2, p 1, k 4, p 9, k 2, p 5, k 1.——7th row, s 1, k 1, tto, n, tto, n, p 2, k 4, tto, k 1, tto, k 4, p 2, k 12.——8th row, k 14, p 11, k 2, p 5, k 1.——9th row, s 1, k 1, tto, n, tto, n, p 2, k 11, p 2, k 12.——10th row, cast off 5, k 8, p 11, k 2, p 5, k 1.——11th row, s 1, k 1, tto, n, tto, n, p 2, s and b, k 7, n, p 2, k 2, tto twice, n, tto twice, n, k 1.——12th row, k 3, p 1, k 2, p 1, k 4, p 9, k 2, p 5, k 1.——13th row, s 1, k 1, tto, n, tto, n, p 2, s and b, k 5, n, p 2, k 9.——14th row, k 11, p 7, k 2, p 5, k 1.——15th row, s 1, k 1, tto, n, tto, n, p 2, s and b, k 3, n, p 2, k 2, tto twice, n, tto twice, n, k 1.——16th row, k 3, p 1, k 2, p 1, k 2, p 1, k 4, p 5, k 2, p 5, k 1.——17th row, s 1, k 1, tto, n, tto, n, p 2, s and b, k 1, n, p 2, k 12.——18th row, k 14, p 3, k 2, p 5, k 1.——19th row, s 1, k 1, tto, n, tto, n, p 2, k 3 together, p 2, k 12.——20th row, cast off 4, k 12, p 5, k 1. Repeat.

1 oz. silk No. 300 makes 2 yds. 9 inches above pattern.

1 oz. silk No. 500 makes 3 yds. 33 inches above pattern.

RULE 46.

LACE EDGING. (Fig. 46.)

Cast on 33 stitches, knit across plain. 1st row, k 2, tto, k 5, tto, n, k 1, n, tto, k 11.——2d row, k 2, tto, k 1, s 1, n, pass s over, k 1, tto, k 17.——3d row, k 2, tto, k 1, n, tto twice, s 1, n, pass s over, k 1, tto, s 1, n, pass s over, tto, k 12.——4th row, k 2, tto, k 1, s 1, n, pass s over, k 1, tto, k 10, in the 2 loops (formed by tto twice in previous row) k 1, p 1, k 1,* k 5.——5th row, k 1, n, tto, n, k 3, n, tto, k 8, tto, n, k 10.——6th row, k 2, tto, k 1, s 1, n, pass s over, k 1, tto, k 17.——7th row, k 1, n, tto, n, k 1, n, tto, k 5, tto, n, k 9.——8th row, k 2, tto, k 1, s 1, n, pass s over, k 1, tto, k 16.——9th row, k 1, n, tto, s 1, n, pass s over, tto, k 1, n, tto twice, s 1, n, pass s over, k 1, tto, n, k 8.——10th row, k 2, tto, k 1, s 1, n, pass s over, k 1, tto, k 5, in the 2 loops (formed by tto twice in previous row) k 1, p 1, k 1,* k 7.——11th row, k 2, tto, k 3, tto, n, k 3, n, tto, k 10.——12th row, k 2, tto, k 1, s 1, n, pass s over, k 1, tto, k 16. Repeat.

1 oz. silk No. 300 makes 2 yds. 0 inches above pattern.

1 oz. silk No. 500 makes 3 yds. 33 inches above pattern.

---

* The two loops formed by tto twice are in this case treated as one long stitch, on which the work k 1, p 1 and k 1 is done.

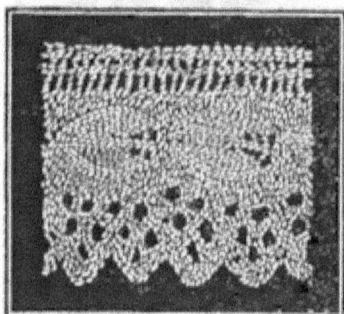
FIG. 45.

FIG. 46.

RULE 47.

LACE EDGING. (Fig. 47.)

Cast on 22 stitches, knit across plain. 1st row, k 3, tto, n, k 3, tto, k 3 together, tto, k 3, tto, k 3 together, tto, k 3, tto, k 2.——2d row, tto, n, tto, k 5, tto, k 1, tto, k 5, tto, k 1, tto, k 6, tto, n, k 1.——3d row, k 3, tto, n, k 7, n, tto, k 1, tto, n, k 3, n, tto, k 1, tto, n, k 1, tto, k 2.——4th row, tto, n, tto, k 1, n, tto, k 3, tto, n, k 1, n, tto, k 3, tto, n, k 5, tto, n, k 1.——5th row, k 3, tto, n, k 7, tto, n, k 1, n, tto, k 3 together, tto, n, k 1, n, tto, n, k 1, tto, k 2.——6th row, tto, n, k 1, slip the second stitch over the last, tto, n, k 1, tto, k 3 together, tto, k 3, tto, k 3 together, tto, k 10, tto, n, k 1.——7th row, k 3, tto, n, k 9, tto, k 1, tto, k 5, tto, k 1, tto, k 1, n, tto, k 1, n.——8th row, tto, n, k 1, slip the second stitch over the last, tto, n, k 3, n, tto, k 1, tto, n, k 3, n, tto, k 3 together, tto, k 6, tto, n, k 1.——9th row, k 3, tto, n, k 2, n, tto, k 3, tto, n, k 1, n, tto, k 3, tto, n, k 1, n, tto, k 1, n.——10th row, tto, n, k 1, slip the second stitch over the last, tto, k 3 together, tto, n, k 1, n, tto, k 3 together, tto, n, k 1, n, tto, n, k 3, tto, n, k 1. Repeat.

1 oz. silk No. 300 makes 2 yds. above pattern.

1 oz. silk No. 500 makes 3 yds. 12 inches above pattern.

RULE 48.

LACE EDGING. (Fig. 48.)

Cast on 19 stitches, knit across plain. 1st row, k 2, tto, n, tto, n, k 6, n, tto, k 3, tto, k 2.——2d row, k 2, tto, k 5, tto, n, k 6, tto, n, tto, n, k 1.——3d row, k 2, tto, n, tto, n, k 4, n, tto, k 1, n, tto, n, k 1, tto, k 2.——4th row, k 2, tto, k 1, n, tto, k 3, tto, n, k 1, tto, n, k 4, tto, n, tto, n, k 1.——5th row, k 2, tto, n, tto, n, k 2, n, tto, k 1, n, tto, k 5, tto, n, k 1, tto, k 2.——6th row, k 2, tto, k 1, n, tto, k 3, tto, n, k 2, tto, n, k 1, tto, n, k 2, tto, n, tto, n, k 1.——7th row, k 2, tto, n, tto, n, k 3, tto, n, k 1, tto, n, k 3, n, tto, k 1, n, tto, k 1, n.——8th row, cast off 1, k 1, tto, n, k 1, tto, n, k 1, n, tto, k 1, n, tto, k 5, tto, n, tto, n, k 1.——9th row, k 2, tto, n, tto, n, k 5, tto, n, k 1, tto, s 1, n, pass s over, tto, k 1, n, k 1, n.——10th row, k 2, tto, n, k 3, n, tto, k 7, tto, n, tto, n, k 1.——11th row, k 2, tto, n, tto, n, k 7, tto, n, k 1, n, tto, k 3.——12th row, cast off 2, k 1, tto, k 3 together, tto, k 9, tto, n, tto, n, k 1. Repeat.

1 oz. silk No. 300 makes 2 yds. above pattern.

1 oz. silk No. 500 makes 3 yds. 12 inches above pattern.

RULE 49.

LACE EDGING. (Fig. 49.)

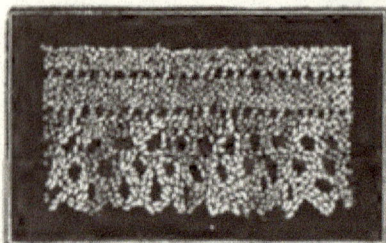

FIG. 49.

Cast on 16 stitches, knit across plain.
1st row, k 3, tto, n, k 2, tto, n, k 1, tto twice, n, tto twice, n, tto twice, n. ——
2d row, k 2, p 1, k 2, p 1, k 2, p 1, k 2, p 1, k 3, p 1, k 3. —— 3d row, k 3, tto, n, k 2, tto, n, k 10. —— 4th row, cast off 3, k 7, p 1, k 3, p 1, k 3. Repeat.

1 oz. silk No 300 makes 3 yds. above pattern.

1 oz. silk No. 500 makes 5 yds. 7 inches above pattern.

———

RULE 50.

LACE EDGING. (Fig. 50.)

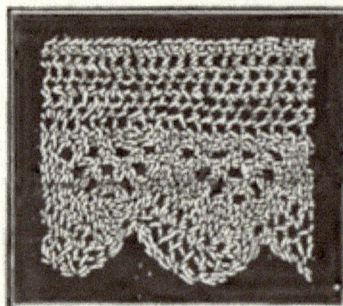

FIG. 50.

Cast on 19 stitches, knit across plain. 1st row, s 1, k 1, tto twice, p n, tto, p n, tto, p n, k 2, tto twice, p n, k 3, tto twice, p n, tto, p n. —— 2d row, tto, p n, tto, p n, k 4, in loop* k 1 and p 1, k 2, tto twice, p n, tto, p n, tto, p n, k 2. —— 3d row, s 1, k 1, tto twice, p n, tto, p n, tto, p n, k 8, tto twice, p n, tto, p n. —— 4th row, tto, p n, tto, p n, k 8, tto twice, p n, tto, p n, tto, p n, k 2. —— 5th row, s 1, k 1, tto twice, p n, tto, p n, tto, p n, k 2, tto twice, p n, tto, p n, k 2, tto twice, p n, tto, p n. —— 6th row, tto, p n, tto, p n, k 3, in loop* k 1 and p 1, k 1, in loop* k 1 and p 1, k 2, tto twice, p n, tto, p n, tto, p n, k 2. —— 7th row, s 1, k 1, tto twice, p n, tto, p n, tto, p n, k 10, tto twice, p n, tto, p n. —— 8th row, tto, p n, tto, p n, k 10, tto twice, p n, tto, p n, tto, p n, k 2. —— 9th row, s 1, k 1, tto twice, p n, tto, p n, tto, p n, k 2, tto twice, p n, tto, p n, tto, p n, k 2, tto twice, p n, tto, p n. —— 10th row, tto, p n, tto, p n, k 3, in loop* k 1 and p 1, k 1, in loop* k 1 and p 1, k 1, in loop* k 1 and p 1, k 2, tto twice, p n, tto, p n, tto, p n, k 2. —— 11th row, s 1, k 1, tto twice, p n, tto, p n, tto, p n, k 13, tto twice, p n, tto, p n. —— 12th row, tto, p n, tto, p n, k 13, tto twice, p n, tto, p n, tto, p n, k 2. —— 13th row, s 1, k 1, tto twice, p n, tto, p n, tto, p n, k 2, tto twice, p n, tto, p n, tto, p n, k 3, tto twice, p n, tto, p n. —— 14th row, tto, p n, tto, p n, k 4, in loop* k 1 and p 1, k 1, in loop* k 1 and p 1, k 1, in loop* k 1 and p 1, k 1, in loop* k 1 and p 1, k 2, tto twice, p n, tto, p n, tto, p n, k 2. —— 15th row, s 1, k 1, tto twice, p n, tto, p n, tto, p n, k 17, tto twice, p n, tto, p n. —— 16th row, tto, p n, tto, p n, k 17, tto twice, p n, tto, p n, tto, p n, k 2. —— 17th row, s 1, k 1, tto twice, p n, tto, p n, tto, p n, k 17, tto twice, p n, tto, p n. —— 18th row, tto, p n, tto, p n, k 7, slip all the other stitches and loops on the right-hand needle over last stitch knit, leaving but one on right-hand needle, then k 10, tto twice, p n, tto, p n, tto, p n, k 2. Repeat.

1 oz. silk No. 300 makes 2 yds. above pattern.

1 oz. silk No. 500 makes 3 yds. 12 inches above pattern.

———

*To the inexperienced or careless knitter, it may cause confusion when told to knit one and purl one on the same loop or stitch. The work is simple, however, and *must* be observed carefully to produce the pattern.

RULE 51.

LACE EDGING. (Fig. 51.)

Cast on 21 stitches, knit across plain. 1st row, k 3, tto, n, tto, n, k 2, k 8, putting thread over four times in knitting each stitch, (not between the stitches) k 2, tto 4 times, k 2.—— 2d row, k 3, p 1, k 1, p 1, k 2, slip the next 4 loops off as 1 stitch, slip the next 4 loops off as 1 stitch, slip the next 4 loops off as 1 stitch, slip the next 4 loops off as 1 stitch, slip the next 4 loops off as 1 stitch, slip the next 4 loops off as 1 stitch, slip the next 4 loops off as 1 stitch, slip the next 4 loops off as 1 stitch. You now have 8 long stitches on the right hand needle. Pass the first 4 of these long stitches over the last 4, and knit the last 4 stitches first, afterwards knitting the first 4. Finish row by k 3, tto, n, tto, n, k 2.—— 3d row, k 3, tto, n, tto, n, k 18.—— 4th row, k 19, tto, n, tto, n, k 2.—— 5th row, k 3, tto, n, tto, n, k 18.—— 6th row, cast off 4, k 14, tto, n, tto, n, k 2. Repeat.

FIG. 51.

NOTE.—The knitting of the second row in this rule is very simple if rightly understood, but great care is to be taken in treating the loops where the thread has been thrown over 4 times. In the beginning of the row it will be observed that the first 2 stitches are regularly formed, while the next 4 are loops, hence in following the directions to k 3, it is necessary to use the first of the loops, taking care not to allow the other three loops to slip off until purled and knitted, each separately as described. We call special attention to this here, because *afterwards*, in same row, the 4 loops are repeatedly slipped off as 1 stitch, and not knitted until crossed. The manner of crossing in this case is to pass the left hand needle into the first 4 stitches from left to right, then pass these over the last 4 towards the left, and knit as described.

1 oz. silk No. 300 makes 1 yd. 28 inches above pattern.

1 oz. silk No. 500 makes 2 yds. 34 inches above pattern.

RULE 52.

LACE EDGING. (Fig. 52.)

Cast on 28 stitches, knit across plain. 1st row, k 2, tto, k 1, s 1, n, pass s over, k 1, tto, k 1, tto, k 1, s and b, p 1, n, k 1, p 1, k 1, s and b, p 1, n, k 1, tto, k 1, tto twice, k 1, tto twice, k 1.—— 2d row, k 2, p 1, k 2, p 1, k 1, p 3, k 1, p 2, k 1, p 2, k 1, p 3, k 8.—— 3d row, k 2, tto, k 1, s 1, n, pass s over, k 1, tto, k 1, tto, k 1, tto, s and b, p 1, n, p 1, s and b, p 1, n, tto, k 1, tto, k 7.—— 4th row, cast off 4, k 2, p 4, k 1, p 1, k 1, p 1, k 1, p 4, k 8.—— 5th row, k 2, tto, k 1, s 1, n, pass s over, k 1, tto, k 1, tto, k 3, tto, s 1, n, pass s over, p 1, s 1, n, pass s over, tto, k 3, tto, k 1, tto twice, k 1, tto twice, k 1.—— 6th row, k 2, p 1, k 2, p 1, k 1, p 6, k 1, p 6, k 8.—— 7th row, k 2, tto, k 1, s 1, n, pass s over, k 1, tto, k 1, tto, k 5, tto, s 1, n, pass s over, tto, k 5, tto, k 7.—— 8th row, cast off 4, k 2, p 15, k 8. Repeat.

FIG. 52.

1 oz. silk No. 300 makes 2 yds. 9 inches above pattern.

1 oz. silk No. 500 makes 3 yds. 33 inches above pattern.

RULE 53.

LACE EDGING. (Fig. 53.)

Cast on 15 stitches, knit across plain. 1st row, k 2, tto, k 1, s 1, n, pass s over, k 1, tto, k 4, tto twice, n, k 2.——2d row, tto, p 2 together, k 2, p 1, k 11.—— 3d row, k 2, tto, k 1, s 1, n, pass s over, k 1, tto, k 2, n, tto twice, k 2, tto twice, k 3.——4th row, tto, p 2 together, k 2, p 1, n, k 1, p 1, k 10.——5th row, k 2, tto, k 1, s 1, n, pass s over, k 1, tto, k 2, n, tto twice, n, k 2, tto twice, k 3.——6th row, tto, p 2 together, n, p 1, k 2, n, p 1, n, k 8.——7th row, k 2, tto, k 1, s 1, n, pass s over, k 1, tto, k 3, tto twice, n, n, tto twice, k 3.——8th row, tto, p 2 together, n, p 1, n, k 1, p 1, n, k 8.——9th row, k 2, tto, k 1, s 1, n, pass s over, k 1, tto, k 4, tto twice, n, tto twice, k 3.——10th row, tto, p 2 together, n, p 1, n, p 1, n, k 9.——11th row, k 2, tto, k 1, s 1, n, pass s over, k 1, tto, k 5, tto twice, n, k 2.——12th row, tto, p 2 together, n, p 1, n, k 10. Repeat.

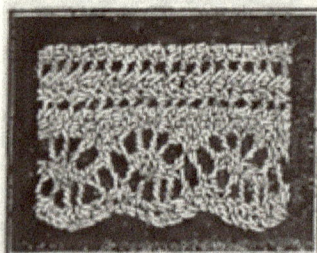

FIG. 53.

1 oz. silk No. 300 makes 3 yds. above pattern.

1 oz. silk No 500 makes 5 yds. 7 inches above pattern.

RULE 54.

LACE EDGING. (Fig. 54.)

Cast on 8 stitches, knit across plain. 1st row, s 1, k 1, tto twice, p n, k 2, tto thrice, k 2.——2d row, k 2, k first loop, p second loop, k third loop, k 2, tto twice, p n, k 2.——3d row, s 1, k 1, tto twice, p n, k 7.——4th row, k 7, tto twice, p n, k 2——5th row, s 1, k 1, tto twice, p n, k 7.——6th row, cast off 3, k 3, tto twice, p n, k 2. Repeat.

FIG. 54.

1 oz. silk No. 300 makes 4 yds. 19 inches above pattern.

1 oz. silk No. 500 makes 7 yds. 32 inches above pattern.

RULE 55.

LACE EDGING. (Fig. 55.)

Cast on 10 stitches, knit across plain. 1st row, k 3, tto, n, tto twice, n, tto twice, n, k 1.——2d row, tto, k 3, p 1, k 2, p 1, k 2, tto, n, k 1.——3d row, k 3, tto, n, k 8.——4th row, cast off 3, k 6, tto, n, k 1. Repeat.

FIG. 55.

1 oz. silk No. 300 makes 4 yds. 19 inches above pattern.

1 oz. silk No. 500 makes 7 yds. 32 inches above pattern.

RULE 56.

LACE EDGING. (Fig. 56.)

Cast on 21 stitches, knit across plain. 1st row, s 1, k 2, tto, n, k 10, tto, n, tto, n, tto, n.——2d row, tto, k 6, p 10, k 1, tto, n, k 2.——3d row, s 1, k 2, tto, n, k 1, tto, n, tto, n, tto, n, k 1, tto, n, k 1, tto, n, tto, n.——4th row, tto, k 7, p 10, k 1, tto, n, k 2.——5th row, s 1, k 2, tto, n, k 1, tto, n, k 4, tto, n, k 1, tto, n, k 2, tto, n, tto, n.——6th row, tto, k 8, p 10, k 1, tto, n, k 2.——7th row, s 1, k 2, tto, n, k 1, tto, n, tto, n, tto, n, tto, n, k 1, tto, n, k 3, tto, n, tto, n.——8th row, tto, k 9, p 10, k 1, tto, n, k 2.——9th row, s 1, k 2, tto, n, k 10, tto, n, k 4, tto, n, tto, n.——10th row, tto, k 21, tto, n, k 2.——11th row, s 1, k 2, tto, n, p 10, tto, n, k 5, tto, n, tto, n.——12th row, tto, k 22, tto, n, k 2.——13th row, s 1, k 2, tto, n, p 10, tto, n, k 6, tto, n, tto, n.——14th row, cast off 6, k 16, tto, n, k 2. Repeat.

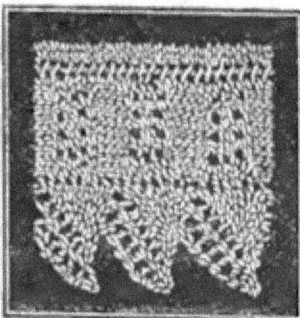

FIG. 56.

1 oz. silk No. 300 makes 1 yd. 23 inches above pattern.

1 oz. silk No. 500 makes 2 yds. 34 inches above pattern.

RULE 57.

LACE EDGING. (Fig. 57.)

Cast on 22 stitches, knit across plain. 1st row, k 3, tto, n, k 1, tto, n, k 2, tto, k 1, tto, n, k 1, n, tto, k 2, tto twice, n, tto twice, n.——2d row, k 2, p 1, k 2, p 1, n, k 1, tto, s 1, n, pass s over, tto, k 3, tto, n, n, tto, n, k 1, tto, n, k 1.——3d row, k 3, tto, n, k 1, tto, n, tto, n, k 1, n, tto, k 1, tto, k 1, n, k 6.——4th row, cast off 2, k 5, tto, k 3, tto, s 1, n, pass s over, tto, k 3, tto, n, k 1, tto, n, k 1. Repeat.

FIG. 57.

1 oz. silk No. 300 makes 2 yds. 9 inches above pattern.

1 oz. silk No. 500 makes 3 yds. 33 inches above pattern.

RULE 58.

LACE EDGING. (Fig. 58.)

Cast on 11 stitches, knit across plain. 1st row, k 3, tto, s and b, k 1, tto, s and b, k 1, tto twice, k 1, tto twice, k 1.——2d row, k 2, p 1, k 2, p 1, k 2, p 1, k 2, p 1, k 3.——3d row, k 3, tto, s and b, k 1, tto, s and b, k 7.——4th row, cast off 4, k 3, p 1, k 2, p 1, k 3. Repeat.

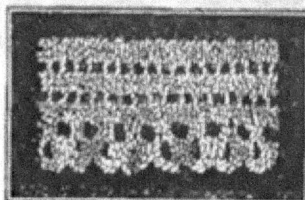

FIG. 58.

1 oz. silk No. 300 makes 3 yds. 14 inches above pattern.

1 oz. silk No. 500 makes 5 yds. 34 inches above pattern.

RULE 59.

LACE EDGING. (Fig. 59.)

Cast on 22 stitches, knit across plain. **1st row,** s 1, k 1, tto, k 1, s 1, n, pass s over, k 1, tto, k 2, tto, n, tto, n, tto, k 9. —— **2d** and every alternate row, s 1, knit the rest plain. —— **3d row,** s 1, k 1, tto, k 1, s 1, n, pass s over, k 1, tto, k 3, tto, n, tto, n, tto, k 9. —— **5th row,** s 1, k 1, tto, k 1, s 1, n, pass s over, k 1, tto, k 4, tto, n, tto, n, tto, k 9. —— **7th row,** s 1, k 1, tto, k 1, s 1, n, pass s over, k 1, tto, k 5, tto, n, tto, n, tto, k 9. —— **9th row,** s 1, k 1, tto, k 1, s 1, n, pass s over, k 1, tto, k 6, tto, n, tto, n, tto, k 9. —— **11th row,** s 1, k 1, tto, k 1, s 1, n, pass s over, k 1, tto, k 7, tto, n, tto, n, tto, k 9. —— **13th row,** s 1, k 1, tto, k 1, s 1, n, pass s over, k 1, tto, k 8, tto, n, tto, n, tto, k 9. —— **15th row,** s 1, k 1, tto, k 1, s 1, n, pass s over, k 1, tto, k 9, tto, n, tto, n, tto, k 9. —— **16th row,** cast off 8, k 21. Repeat.

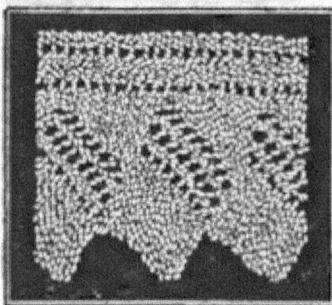

1 oz. silk, No. 300 makes 1 yd. 28 inches above pattern.
1 oz. silk No. 500 makes 2 yds. 34 inches above pattern.

FIG. 59.

RULE 60.

LACE EDGING. (Fig. 60.)

Cast on 19 stitches, knit across plain. **1st row,** s 1, k 1, tto twice, p n, k 1, tto k 1, s 1, n, pass s over, k 1, tto, k 1, tto twice, p n, k 1, tto twice, n, tto twice, n, k 1. —— **2d row,** k 3, p 1, k 2, p 1, k 1, tto twice, p n, k 7, tto twice, p n, k 2. —— **3d row,** s 1, k 1, tto twice, p n, k 1, tto, k 1, s 1, n, pass s over, k 1, tto, k 1, tto twice, p n, k 3, tto twice, n, tto twice, n, k 1. —— **4th row,** k 3, p 1, k 2, p 1, k 3, tto twice, p n, k 7, tto twice, p n, k 2. —— **5th row,** s 1, k 1, tto twice, p n, k 1, tto, k 1, s 1, n, pass s over, k 1, tto, k 1, tto twice, p n, k 5, tto twice, n, tto twice, n, k 1. —— **6th row,** k 3, p 1, k 2, p 1, k 5, tto twice, p n, k 7, tto twice, p n, k 2. —— **7th row,** s 1, k 1, tto twice, p n, k 1, tto, k 1, s 1, n, pass s over, k 1, tto, k 1, tto twice, p n, k 7, tto twice, n, tto twice, n, k 1. —— **8th row,** k 3, p 1, k 2, p 1, k 7, tto twice, p n, k 7, tto twice, p n, k 2 —— **9th row,** s 1, k 1, tto twice, p n, k 1, tto, k 1, s 1, n, pass s over, k 1, tto, k 1, tto twice, p n, k 9, tto twice, n, tto twice, n, k 1. —— **10th row,** cast off 10, k 5, tto twice, p n, k 7, tto twice, p n, k 2. Repeat.

1 oz. silk No. 300 makes 1 yd. 28 inches above pattern.
1 oz. silk No. 500 makes 2 yds. 34 inches above pattern.

FIG. 60.

RULE 6I.

LACE EDGING. (Fig. 61.)

Cast on 18 stitches, knit across plain. 1st row, k 12, tto, n, k 1, tto, k 3. —— 2d row, k 10, tto, n, k 1, tto, n, k 4. —— 3d row, k 13, tto, n, k 1, tto, k 3. —— 4th row, k 12, tto, n, k 1, tto, n, k 3 —— 5th row, k 14, tto, n, k 1, tto, k 3. —— 6th row, k 14, tto, n, k 1, tto, n, k 2. —— 7th row, k 15, tto, n, k 1, tto, k 3. —— 8th row, k 16, tto, n, k 1, tto, n, k 1. —— 9th row, k 22. —— 10th row, k 1, n, k 1, tto, n, k 1, tto, n, k 13. —— 11th row, k 3, tto, n, k 1, tto, n, k 13. —— 12th row, k 1, n, k 1, tto, n, k 1, tto, n, k 12. —— 13th row, k 4, tto, n, k 1, tto, n, k 11. —— 14th row, k 1, n, k 1, tto, n, k 1, tto, n, k 11. —— 15th row, k 5, tto, n, k 1, tto, n, k 9. —— 16th row, k 1, n, k 1, tto, n, k 1, tto, n, k 10. —— 17th row, k 6, tto, n, k 1, tto, n, k 7. —— 18th row, k 18. Repeat.

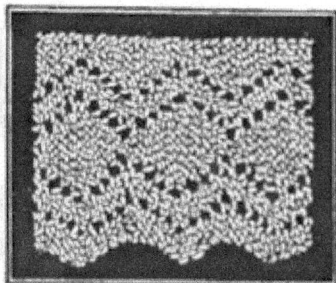

FIG. 61.

1 oz. silk No. 300 makes 3 yds. 14 inches above pattern.

1 oz. silk No. 500 makes 5 yds. 34 inches above pattern.

RULE 62.

LACE INSERTION. (Fig. 62.)

Cast on 13 stitches, knit across plain. 1st row, k 1, tto, n, k 3, tto, n, k 3, tto, n. —— 2d, 4th and 6th rows, k 3, p 7, k 3. —— 3d row, k 1, tto, n, k 1, n, tto, k 1, tto, n, k 2, tto, n. —— 5th row, k 1, tto, n, n, tto, k 3, tto, n, k 1, tto, n. —— 7th row, k 1, tto, s 1, n, pass s over, tto, k 5, tto, n, tto, n. —— 8th row, same as 2d. Repeat.

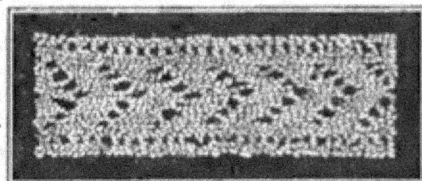

FIG. 62.

1 oz. silk No. 300 makes 4 yds. 19 inches above pattern.

1 oz. silk No. 500 makes 7 yds. 32 inches above pattern.

RULE 63.

LACE EDGING. (Fig. 63.)

Cast on 9 stitches, knit across plain. 1st row, k 3, n, tto, n, tto, k 1, tto, k 1. —— 2d and every alternate row, knit plain. —— 3d row, k 2, n, tto, n, tto, k 3, tto, k 1. —— 5th row, k 1, n, tto, n, tto, k 5, tto, k 1. —— 7th row, k 3, tto, n, tto, n, k 1, n, tto, n. —— 9th row, k 4, tto, n, tto, k 3 together, tto, n. —— 11th row, k 5, tto, k 3 together, tto, n. —— 12th row, knit plain. Repeat.

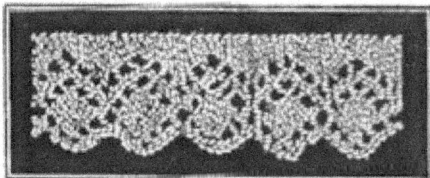

FIG. 63.

1 oz. silk No. 300 makes 4 yds. 19 inches above pattern.

1 oz. silk No. 500 makes 7 yds. 32 inches above pattern.

RULE 64.

LACE EDGING. (Fig. 64.)

Cast on 17 stitches, knit across plain. 1st row, k 2, tto, n, k 1, tto, n, k 1, s and b, tto, k 3, tto twice, n, tto twice, k 2.——2d row, k 3, p 1, k 2, p 1, k 3, p 5, k 5——3d row, k 2, tto, n, k 1, tto, n, k 1, s and b, tto, k 10.——4th row, k 2, tto twice, n, k 1, n, tto twice, n, k 2, p 3, k 6.——5th row, k 2, tto, n, k 2, tto, k 3 together, tto, k 4, p 1, k 4, p 1, k 2.——6th row, k 12, p 3, k 6. ——7th row, k 2, tto, n, n, tto, k 3, tto, n, k 2, tto twice, s 1, k 3 together, pass s over, tto twice, n, n.——8th row, k 3, p 1, k 2, p 1, k 3, p 5, k 5.

FIG. 64.

9th row, k 2, tto, n, k 1, tto, n, k 1, s and b, tto, k 10.——10th row, cast off 3, k 6, p 1, tto, n, p 1, k 6. Repeat.

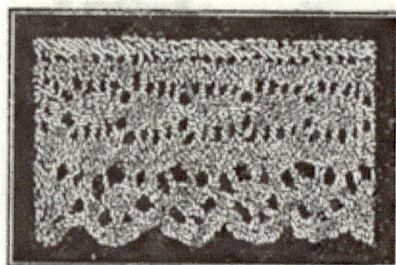

1 oz. silk No. 300 makes 2 yds. 9 inches above pattern.
1 oz. silk No. 500 makes 3 yds. 33 inches above pattern.

RULE 65.

LACE INSERTION. (Fig. 65.)

Cast on 15 stitches, knit across plain. 1st row, k 2, tto, n, k 1, tto, n, k 1, s and b, tto, k 1, n, tto, k 2.——2d, 4th, 6th and 8th rows, k 3, p 3, k 3, p 3, k 3.——3d row, k 2, tto n, k 1, tto, n, k 1, s and b, tto, k 1, n, tto, k 2.——5th row, k 2, tto, n, k 2, tto, k 3 together, tto, k 2, n, tto, k 2.——7th row, k 2, tto, n, n, tto, k 3, tto, n, n, tto, k 2.—— 9th row, k 2, tto, n, k 1, tto, n, k 1, s and b, tto, k 1, n, tto, k 2.——

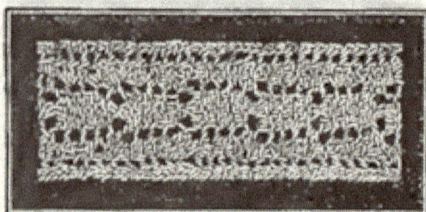

FIG. 65.

10th row, same as 2d. Repeat.

1 oz. silk No. 300 makes 3 yds. 14 inches above pattern.
1 oz. silk No. 500 makes 5 yds. 34 inches above pattern.

RULE 66.

LACE EDGING. (Fig. 66.)

Cast on 5 stitches, knit across plain. 1st row, k 1, tto, k 2 together, tto twice, k 2.——2d row, k 2, k 1 loop, p 1 loop, k 3.——3d row, k 1, tto, k 2 together, k 4——4th row, cast off 2, k 4. Repeat.

1 oz. silk No. 300 makes 7 yds. 35 inches above pattern.

FIG. 66.

1 oz. silk No. 500 makes 13 yds. 33 inches above pattern.

RULE 67.

LACE EDGING. (Fig. 67.)

Cast on 8 stitches, knit across plain. 1st row, tto, n, k 3, tto, n, k 1.——2d row, s 1, k 2, tto, n, k 1, tto, k 2 ——3d row, tto, n, k 4, tto, n, k 1.——4th row, s 1, k 2, tto, n, k 2, tto, k 2.——5th row, tto, n, k 2, tto, n, k 1, tto, n, k 1.——6th row, s 1, k 2, tto, n, on tto work 1 k and 1 p, n, tto, k 2.——7th row, tto, n, k 6, tto, n, k 1.——8th row, s 1, k 2, tto, n, k 2, tto, k 1, tto, n, k 1 ——9th row, tto, n, k 2, on tto work 1 p and 1 k, n, k 2, tto, n, k 1.——

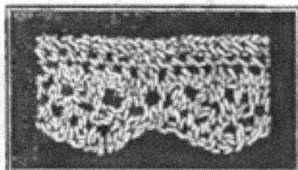

FIG. 67.

10th row, s 1, k 2, tto, n, k 2, n, tto, n, k 1.——11th row, tto, n, k 1, n, tto, n, k 1, tto, n, k 1.——12th row, s 1, k 2, tto, n, on tto work 1 k and 1 p, k 1, tto, n, k 1.——13th row, tto, n, k 1, n, n, k 1, tto, n, k 1.——14th row, s 1, k 2, tto, n, k 1, tto, n, k 1.——15th row, tto, n, k 1, n, k 1, tto, n, k 1.——16th row, s 1, k 2, tto, n, tto, n, k 1. Repeat.

1 oz. silk No. 300 makes 4 yds. 29 inches above pattern.

1 oz. silk No. 500 makes 8 yds. 14 inches above pattern.

RULE 68.

LACE EDGING. (Fig. 68.)

Cast on 14 stitches, knit across plain. 1st row, s 1, k 1, tto, s and b, k 2, tto, n, tto, n, tto, n, tto, k 2.——2d and every alternate row, knit plain till there are 3 left, then tto, s and b, k 1.——3d row, s 1, k 1, tto, s and b, k 3, tto, n, tto, n, tto, n, tto, k 2.——5th row, s 1, k 1, tto, s and b, k 4, tto, n, tto, n, tto, n, tto, k 2. —— 7th row, s 1, k 1, tto, s and b, k 5, tto, n, tto, n, tto, n, tto, k 2.——9th row, s 1, k 1, tto, s and b, k 6, tto, n, tto, n, tto, n, tto, k 2.——11th row, s 1, k 1, tto, s and b, k 7, tto, n, tto, n, tto, n, tto, k 2.——13th row, s 1, k 1, tto, s and b, k 3, tto, n, k 3, tto, n, tto, n, tto, n, tto, k 2.——15th row, s 1, k 1, tto, s and b, k 2, tto, n, tto, n, k 3, tto, n, tto, n, tto, n, tto, k 2.——17th row, s 1, k 1, tto, s and b, k 1, tto, n, tto,

FIG. 68.

n, tto, n, k 3, tto, n, tto, n, tto, n, tto, k 2.——19th row, s 1, k 1, tto, s and b, k 2, tto, n, tto, n, k 2, n, tto, n, tto, n, tto, n, tto, n, k 1.——21st row, s 1, k 1, tto, s and b, k 3, tto, n, k 2, n, tto, n, tto, n, tto, n, tto, n, k 1.——23d row, s 1, k 1, tto, s and b, k 6, n, tto, n, tto, n, tto, n, tto, n, k 1.——25th row, s 1, k 1, tto, s and b, k 5, n, tto, n, tto, n, tto, n, tto, n, k 1.——27th row, s 1, k 1, tto, s and b, k 4, n, tto, n, tto, n, tto, n, tto, n, k 1.——29th row, s 1, k 1, tto, s and b, k 3, n, tto, n, tto, n, tto, n, tto, n, k 1.——31st row, s 1, k 1, tto, s and b, k 2, n, tto, n, tto, n, tto, n, tto, n, k 1.——33d row, s 1, k 1, tto, s and b, k 1, n, tto, n, tto, n, tto, n, k 1.——35th row, s 1, k 1, tto, s and b, n, tto, n, tto, n, tto, n, tto, n, k 1. Repeat.

1 oz. silk No. 300 makes 2 yds. 9 inches above pattern.

1 oz. silk No. 500 makes 3 yds. 33 inches above pattern.

RULE 69.

LACE EDGING. (Fig. 69.)

Cast on 10 stitches, knit across plain. 1st row, s 1, k 1, tto, n, tto, n, tto thrice, n, tto twice, p 2 together.—— 2d row, tto twice, p 2 together, k 2, p 1, in next loop k 1 and p 1 †, k 1, p 1, k 1, p 1, k 2. —— 3d row, s 1, k 1, tto, n, k 1, tto, n, k 4, tto twice, p 2 together. —— 4th row, tto twice, p 2 together, k 5, p 1, k 2, p 1, k 2 —— 5th row, s 1, k 1, tto, n, k 2, tto, n, k 3, tto twice, p 2 together. —— 6th row, tto twice, p 2 together, k 4, p 1, k 3, p 1, k 2.—— 7th row,

FIG. 69.

s 1, k 1, tto, n, k 3, tto, n, k 2, tto twice, p 2 together. —— 8th row, tto twice, p 2 together, k 3, p 1, k 4, p 1, k 2.—— 9th row, s 1, k 1, tto, n, k 4, tto, n, k 1, tto twice, p 2 together.—— 10th row, tto twice, p 2 together, k 2, p 1, k 5, p 1, k 2. 11th row, s 1, k 1, tto, n, k 5, tto, n, tto twice, p 2 together. —— 12th row, cast off 3 stitches, place the stitch remaining on the right-hand needle on the left-hand needle, then tto twice, p 2 together, k 5, p 1, k 2. Repeat.

1 oz. silk No. 300 makes 4 yds. 2 inches above pattern.

1 oz. silk No. 500 makes 7 yds. 4 inches above pattern.

RULE 70.

LACE EDGING. (Fig. 70.)

Cast on 13 stitches, knit across plain. 1st row, k 2, tto twice, p 2 together, k 1, tto, n, tto, n, tto, n, tto, k 2. —— 2d row, k 10, tto twice, p 2 together, k 2. —— 3d row, k 2, tto twice, p 2 together, k 2, tto, n, tto, n, tto, n, tto, k 2. —— 4th row, k 11, tto twice, p 2 together, k 2. —— 5th row, k 2, tto twice, p 2 together, k 3, tto, n, tto, n, tto, n, tto, k 2 —— 6th row, k 12, tto twice, p 2 together, k 2.—— 7th row, k 2, tto twice, p 2 together, k 4, tto, n, tto, n, tto, n, tto,

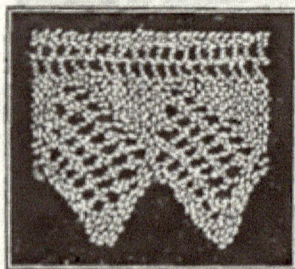

FIG. 70.

k 2.—— 8th row, k 13, tto twice, p 2 together, k 2.—— 9th row, k 2, tto twice, p 2 together, k 5, tto, n, tto, n, tto, k 2.—— 10th row, k 14, tto twice, p 2 together, k 2. —— 11th row, k 2, tto twice, p 2 together, k 6, tto, n, tto, n, tto, n, tto, k 2.—— 12th row, k 15, tto twice, p 2 together, k 2. —— 13th row, k 2, tto twice, p 2 together, k 7, tto, n, tto, n, tto, n, tto, k 2 —— 14th row, k 16, tto twice, p 2 together, k 2. —— 15th row, k 2, tto twice, p 2 together, k 16.—— 16th row, cast off 7 stitches, k 8, tto twice, p 2 together, k 2. Repeat.

1 oz. silk No. 300 makes 2 yds. 23 inches above pattern.

1 oz. silk No. 500 makes 4 yds. 21 inches above pattern.

† To knit 1 and purl 1 in same loop, may seem difficult. It is easy, however. First to k 1, draw the thread through, but do not slip off the loop from needle until you have brought the thread forward and purled 1, thus making two new stitches on the old loop.

RULE 71.

LACE EDGING. (Fig. 71.)

Cast on 14 stitches, knit across plain. 1st row, k 4, tto, n, k 2, tto twice, n, k 1, tto twice, n, k 1.——2d row, k 3, p 1, k 3, p 1, k 3, p 1, k 8.——3d row, k 4, tto, n, k 10.——4th and 8th rows, knit plain.——5th row, k 4, tto, n, k 1, tto twice, n, k 1, tto twice, n, k 1, tto twice, n, k 1.—— 6th row, k 3, p 1, k 3, p 1, k 3, p 1, k 7.——7th row, k 4, tto, n, k 13.——9th row, k 4, tto, n, k 5, tto twice, n, k 1, tto twice, n, k 1, n.——10th row, k 4, p 1, k 3, p 1, k 11.——11th row, k 4, tto, n, k 12, n.——12th row, cast off 5 stitches and knit 13 plain. Repeat.

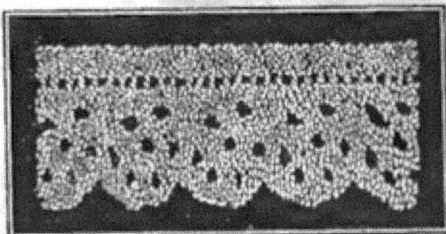

FIG. 71.

1 oz. silk No. 300 makes 2 yds. 35 inches above pattern.

1 oz. silk No. 500 makes 5 yds. 6 inches above pattern.

RULE 72.

LACE EDGING. (Fig. 72.)

Cast on 16 stitches, knit across plain. 1st row, s 1, k 2, tto, n, k 1, tto twice, n, k 8.——2d row, s 1, k 8, k 1 loop, p 1 loop, k 3, tto, n, k 1.——3d row, s 1, k 2, tto, n, k 7, tto, n, k 3. ——4th row, s 1, k 13, tto, n, k 1. ——5th row, s 1, k 2, tto, n, k 1, tto twice, n, tto twice, n, k 1, tto, n, tto, n, k 2. —— 6th row, s 1, k 7, k 1 loop, p 1 loop, k 1, k 1 loop, p 1 loop, k 3, tto, n, k 1. —— 7th row, s 1, k 2, tto, n, k 9, tto, n, k 3 ——

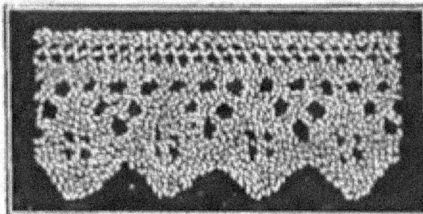

FIG. 72.

8th row, s 1, k 15, tto, n, k 1.——9th row, s 1, k 2, tto, n, k 1, tto twice, n, tto twice, n, tto twice, n, k 7.——10th row, s 1, k 7, k 1 loop, p 1 loop, k 1, k 1 loop, p 1 loop, k 1, k 1 loop, p 1 loop, k 3, tto, n, k 1.——11th row, s 1, k 2, tto, n, k 17. ——12th row, s 1, cast off 6, k 12, tto, n, k 1. Repeat.

1 oz. silk No. 300 makes 2 yds. 23 inches above pattern.

1 oz. silk No. 500 makes 4 yds. 21 inches above pattern.

RULE 73

LACE EDGING. (Fig. 73.)

Cast on 3 stitches, knit across plain. 1st row, k 1, tto twice, k 2.——2d row, k 2, k 1 loop, p 1 loop, k 1.——3d row, k 5.——4th row, cast off 2, k 2. Repeat.

1 oz. silk No. 300 makes 12½ yds. above pattern.

1 oz. silk No. 500 makes 21 yds. 26 inches above pattern.

FIG. 73.

RULE 74.

LACE EDGING. (Fig. 74.)

Cast on 12 stitches, knit across plain. 1st row, k 2, tto twice, n, k 6, tto twice, p 2 together.——2d row, tto, p 2 together, k 7, k 1 loop, p 1 loop, k 2.——3d row, k 11, tto twice, p 2 together.——4th row, tto, p 2 together, k 11.——5th row, k 2, tto twice, n, tto twice, n, k 5, tto twice, p 2 together.——6th row, tto, p 2 together, k 6, k 1 loop, p 1 loop, k 1, k 1 loop, p 1 loop, k 2.——7th row, k 13, tto twice, p 2 together.——8th row, tto, p 2 together, k 13.——9th row, k 2, tto twice, n, tto twice, n, tto twice, n, k 5, tto twice, p 2 together.——10th row, tto, p 2 together, k 6, k 1 loop, p 1 loop, k 1, k 1 loop, p 1 loop, k 1, k 1 loop, p 1 loop, k 2.——11th row, k 11, take 11th back on left-hand needle and slip 6 stitches over that stitch, tto twice, p 2 together.——12th row, tto, p 2 together, k 10. Repeat.

1 oz. silk No. 300 makes 4 yds. 19 inches above pattern.
1 oz. silk No. 500 makes 7 yds. 32 inches above pattern.

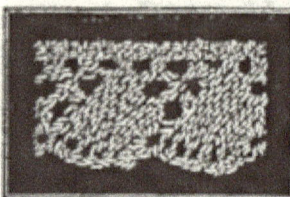

FIG. 74.

RULE 75.

LACE EDGING. (Fig. 75.)

Cast on 9 stitches, knit across plain. 1st row, s 1, k 2, tto, n, k 1, tto twice, n, k 1.——2d row, k 2, k 1 loop, p 1 loop, k 3, tto, n, k 1.——3d row, s 1, k 2, tto, n, k 5.——4th row, k 7, tto, n, k 1.——5th row, s 1, k 2, tto, n, k 1, tto twice, n, tto twice, n.——6th row, k 1, k 1 loop, p 1 loop, k 1, k 1 loop, p 1 loop, k 3, tto, n, k 1.——7th row, s 1, k 2, tto, n, k 7.——8th row, cast off 3, k 5, tto, n, k 1. Repeat.

1 oz. silk No. 300 makes 4 yds. 16 inches above pattern.
1 oz. silk No. 500 makes 7 yds. 28 inches above pattern.

FIG. 75.

RULE 76.

LACE EDGING. (Fig. 76.)

Cast on 13 stitches, knit across plain. 1st row, p 3, k 8, p 2.——2d row, s and b, tto twice, p 8, tto, s 1, n, pass s over.——3d row, on first stitch k 1 and p 1, then k 10, p 1.——4th row, s 1, k 1, tto twice, p 2 together, p 4, p 2 together, tto, k 3.——5th row, on first stitch, k 1 and p 1, then p 3, k 6, p 3.——6th row, s 1, k 2, tto twice, p 2 together, p 2, p 2 together, tto, k 5.——7th row, on first stitch k 1 and p 1, then p 5, k 4, p 4.——8th row, s 1, k 3, tto twice, p 2 together twice, tto, k 1, n, tto twice, n, k 2.——9th row, s 1, p 2, k 1 loop, p 1 loop, p 3, k 2, p 5.——10th row, s 1, k 1, n, tto twice, p 4, tto, n, k 3, n.——11th row, s 1, p 4, k 6, p 3.——12th row, s 1, n, tto twice, p 6, tto, n, k 1, n. Repeat.

1 oz. silk No. 300 makes 3 yds. 14 inches above pattern.
1 oz. silk No. 500 makes 5 yds. 34 inches above pattern.

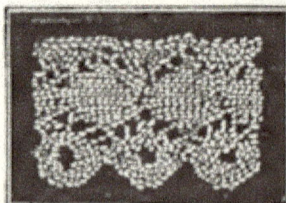

FIG. 76.

RULE 77.

LACE EDGING. (Fig. 77.)

Cast on 12 stitches, knit across plain. 1st row, s 1, k 1, tto, n, tto, n, tto, n, tto, k 4.——2d and every alternate row, knit plain. ——3d row, s 1, k 1, tto, n, tto, n, tto, n, tto, k 5.——5th row, s 1, k 1, tto, n, tto, n, tto, n, tto, k 6.——7th row, s 1, k 1, tto, n, tto, n, tto, n, tto, k 7.——9th row, s 1, k 1, tto, n, tto, n, tto, n, tto, k 8.——11th row, s 1, k 1, tto, n, tto, n, tto, n, tto, k 9 ——13th row, s 1, k 1, tto, n, tto, n, tto, n, tto, k 10.——15th row, all plain.——17th row, s 1, n, tto, n, tto, n, tto, n, tto, n, k 8.——19th row, s 1, n, tto, n, tto, n, tto, n, tto, n, k 7.——21st row, s 1, n, tto, n, tto, n, tto, n, tto, n, k 6.

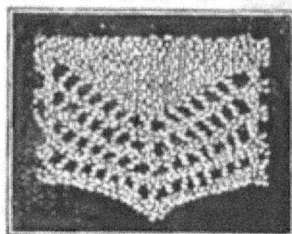

FIG. 77.

——23d row, s 1, n, tto, n, tto, n, tto, n, tto, n, k 5 ——25th row, s 1, n, tto, n, tto, n, tto, n, tto, n, k 4.——27th row, s 1, n, tto, n, tto, n, tto, n, tto, n, k 3.——29th row, s 1, n, tto, n, tto, n, tto, n, tto, n, k 2.——30th, 31st and 32d rows, all plain. Repeat.

1 oz. silk No. 300 makes 2 yds. 16 inches above pattern.

1 oz. silk No. 500 makes 4 yds. 9 inches above pattern.

RULE 78.

LACE EDGING. (Fig. 78.)

Cast on 12 stitches, knit across plain. 1st row, s 1, k 1, tto, n, p 1, k 4, tto, n, tto, k 1.——2d row, tto, purl across.——3d row, s 1, k 1, tto, n, p 1, n, k 2, tto, n, tto, k 3.——4th, 6th, 8th and 10th rows, same as 2d.——5th row, s 1, k 1, tto, n, p 1, n, k 1, tto, n, tto, k 5.——7th row, s 1, k 1, tto, n, p 1, n, tto, n, tto, k 7.——9th row, s 1, k 1, tto, n, n, tto, n, tto, k 9.——11th row, s 1, k 1, tto, n, k 1, tto, n, tto, k 3, s and b, p 1, n, k 3.——12th, 14th, 16th, 18th

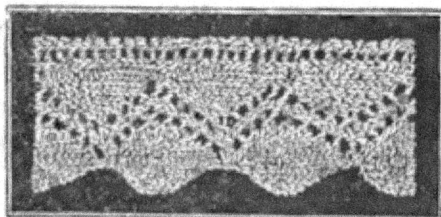

FIG. 78.

and 20th rows, purl across ——13th row, s 1, k 1, tto, n, k 2, tto, n, tto, k 2, s and b, p 1, n, k 2.——15th row, s 1, k 1, tto, n, k 3, tto, n, tto, k 1, s and b, p 1, n, k 1.——17th row, s 1, k 1, tto, n, k 4, tto, n, tto, s and b, p 1, n.——19th row, s 1, k 1, tto, n, k 6, tto, n, s 1, n, pass s over. Repeat.

1 oz. silk No. 300 makes 3 yds. 14 inches above pattern.

1 oz. silk No. 500 makes 5 yds. 34 inches above pattern.

RULE 79.

LACE EDGING. (Fig. 79.)

Cast on 12 stitches, knit across plain. 1st row, tto, k 2, tto, n, k 8.——2d row, s 1, k 1, tto, k 3 together, tto, k 2, n, tto, k 4.——3d row, tto, k 5, tto, n, k 6.——4th row, s 1, k 1, tto, k 3 together, tto, n, tto, k 7.——5th row, s 1, k 4, n, tto, k 7.——6th row, s 1, k 1, tto, k 3 together, tto, k 3, tto, n, k 2, n.——7th row, s 1, k 1, n, tto, k 9.——8th row, s 1, k 1, tto, k 3 together, tto, k 5, tto, k 3 together. Repeat.

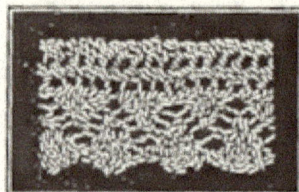

FIG. 79.

1 oz. silk No. 300 makes 3 yds. 22 inches above pattern.

1 oz. silk No. 500 makes 6 yds. 11 inches above pattern.

RULE 80.

LACE EDGING. (Fig. 80.)

Cast on 7 stitches, knit across plain. 1st row, s 1, k 1, tto, n, tto, k 1, tto, k 2.——2d row, tto, n, p 4, k 1, tto, n.——3d row, s 1, k 1, tto, n, tto, k 3, tto, k 2.——4th row, tto, n, p 6, k 1, tto, n.——5th row, s 1, k 1, tto, n, tto, k 1, tto, s 1, n, pass s over, tto, k 1, tto, k 2.——6th row, tto, n, p 8, k 1, tto, n.——7th row, s 1, k 1, tto, n, tto, k 3, tto, k 1, tto, k 3, tto, k 2.——8th row, tto, n, p 12, k 1, tto, n.——9th row, s 1, k 1, tto, s 1, n, pass s over, tto, s 1, n, pass s over, tto, k 3, tto, s 1, n, pass s over, tto, n, k 1.——10th row, tto, n, p 10, k 1, tto, n.——11th row, s 1, k 1, tto, s 1, n, pass s over, n, tto, s 1, n, pass s over, tto, s 1, n, pass s over, n.——12th row, tto, n, p 5, k 1, tto, n.——13th row, s 1, k 1, tto, s 1, k 3 together, pass s over, tto, s 1, n, pass s over, k 1.——14th row, tto, n, p 2, k 1, tto, n. Repeat.

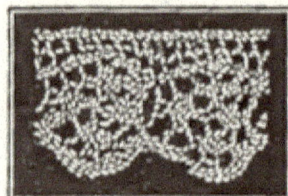

FIG. 80.

1 oz. silk No. 300 makes 4 yds. 1 inch above pattern.

1 oz. silk No. 500 makes 7 yds. above pattern.

RULE 81.

LACE INSERTION. (Fig. 81.)

Cast on 13 stitches, knit across plain. 1st row, s 1, k 3, n, tto, k 1, tto, n, k 4.——2d and every alternate row, knit plain.——3d row, s 1, k 2, n, tto, k 3, tto, n, k 3.——5th row, s 1, k 1, n, tto, k 5, tto, n, k 2.——7th row, s 1, k 3, tto, n, k 1, n, tto, k 4.——9th row, s 1, k 4, tto, k 3 together, tto, k 5.——10th row, knit plain. Repeat.

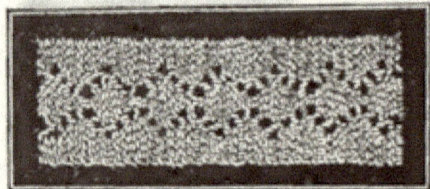

FIG. 81.

1 oz. silk No. 300 makes 4 yds. 19 inches above pattern.

1 oz. silk No. 500 makes 7 yds. 32 inches above pattern.

RULE 82.

LACE EDGING. (Fig. 82.)

Cast on 11 stitches, knit across plain. **1st row,** s 1, k 4, tto, s 1, k 2 together, pass a stitch over, tto, k 1, k 2 together crossed.——
2d row, s 1, k 4, n, k 3.——**3d row,** s 1, k 3, tto twice, p 3, tto, k 2.—— **4th row,** s 1, k 6, n, k 2.
——**5th row,** s 1, k 2, tto, s 1, k 2 together, pass a stitch over, tto 3 times, n, tto, k 2.——**6th row,** s 1, k 1, p 2, on the 3 tto, (k 1, p 1, k 1,) then p 1, k 1, n, k 1.——**7th row,** s 1, k 1, tto, k 7, tto, k 2.——**8th row,** s 1, k 2, p 7, k 3.——**9th row,** s 1, k 2, tto, n, k 3, n, tto, k 1, k 2 together crossed.——**10th row,** s 1, k 2, p 5, k 4.——**11th row,** s 1, k 3, tto, n, k 1, n, tto, k 1, k 2 together crossed.——**12th row,** s 1, k 2, p 3, k 5. Repeat.

FIG. 82.

1 oz. silk No. 300 makes 4 yds. 2 inches above pattern.

1 oz. silk No. 500 makes 7 yds. 4 inches above pattern.

RULE 83.

LACE EDGING. (Fig. 83.)

Cast on 18 stitches, knit across plain. **1st row,** knit across plain.——**2d row,** p 14, pay no attention to the remaining stitches.——**3d row,** slip off the first of the 14 stitches on the right-hand needle with the four, then k 9, n, tto twice, k 2.——**4th row,** p 14, making one stitch of the two loops.——**5th row,** s 1, k 13, this ends one quill. For quill No. 2: **6th row,** k 18.——**7th row,** k 4, p 14. ——**8th row,** k 1, n, tto twice, k 11.——**9th row,** s 1, p 13.——**10th row,** k 18. Continue knitting quills, Nos. 1 and 2.

FIG. 83.

1 oz. silk No. 300 makes 1 yd. 9 inches above pattern.

1 oz. silk No. 500 makes 2 yds. 6 inches above pattern.

RULE 84.

LACE EDGING. (Fig. 84.)

Cast on 16 stitches, knit across plain. **1st row,** s 1, tto, n, tto, n, p 10, on the last stitch, k 1 and p 1.——**2d row,** knit plain. **3d row,** s 1, tto, n, tto, n, p 11, on the last stitch, p 1 and k 1.——**4th row,** knit plain.——**5th row,** s 1, tto, n, tto, n, p 1, 6 times alternately tto and p 2 together.——**6th row,** knit plain.—— **7th row,** s 1, tto, n, tto, n, p 11, p 2 together. ——**8th row,** knit plain.——**9th row,** s 1, tto, n, tto, n, p 10, p 2 together.——**10th row,** knit plain.——**11th row,** s 1, tto, n, tto, n, p 1, k 10.——**12th row,** s 1, p 9, pay no attention to remaining stitch, turn.——**13th row,**

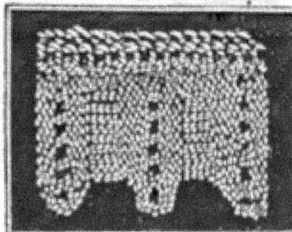

FIG. 84.

s 1, k 9.——**14th and 15th rows,** like 12th and 13th.——**16th row,** s 1, p 9, k 6. Repeat.

1 oz. silk No. 300 makes 2 yds. 26 inches above pattern.

1 oz. silk No. 500 makes 4 yds. 26 inches above pattern.

RULE 85.

LACE INSERTION. (Fig. 85.)

Cast on 19 stitches and purl across. 1st row, s 1, p 1, n, k 2, tto, n, tto, k 3, tto, n, tto, k 2, n, p 1, k 1.——2d and every alternate row, purl across.——3d row, s 1, p 1, n, k 1, tto, n, tto, k 5, tto, n, tto, k 1, n, p 1, k 1.——5th row, s 1, p 1, n, tto, n, tto, k 7, tto, n, tto, n, p 1, k 1.——7th row, s 1, n, tto, n, tto, k 9, tto, n, tto, n, k 1.——9th row, s 1, k 1, tto, n, tto, k 3, s and b, p 1, n, k 3, tto, n, tto, k 2.——11th row, s 1, k 2, tto, n, tto, k 2, s and b, p 1, n, k 2, tto, n, tto, k 3.——13th row, s 1, k 3, tto, n, tto, k 1, s and b, p 1, n, k 1, tto, n, tto, k 4.——15th row, s 1, k 4, tto, n, tto, s and b, p 1, n, tto, n. tto, k 5.——17th row, s 1, k 5, tto, n, tto, s 1, n, pass s over, tto, n, tto, k 6.——18th row, purl across. Repeat.

1 oz. silk No. 300 makes 2 yds. 9 inches above pattern.
1 oz. silk No. 500 makes 3 yds. 33 inches above pattern.

FIG. 85.

RULE 86.

LACE EDGING. (Fig. 86.)

Cast on 15 stitches, knit across plain. 1st row, s 1, k 1, tto twice, p 2 together, k 1, tto, n, k 3, tto twice, p 2 together, k 1, tto, k 2.——2d row, k 2, p 1, k 1, tto twice, p 2 together, k 4, p 1, k 1, tto twice, p 2 together, k 2.——3d row, s 1, k 1, tto twice, p 2 together, k 2, tto, n, k 2, tto twice, p 2 together, k 2, tto, k 2.——4th row, k 2, p 1, k 2, tto twice, p 2 together, k 3, p 1, k 2, tto twice, p 2 together, k 2.——5th row, s 1, k 1, tto twice, p 2 together, k 3, tto, n, k 1, tto twice, p 2 together, k 3, tto, k 2.——6th row, k 2, p 1, k 3, tto twice, p 2 together, k 2, p 1, k 3, tto twice, p 2 together, k 2.——7th row, s 1, k 1, tto twice, p 2 together, k 4, tto, n, tto twice, p 2 together, k 6.——8th row, cast off 3, k 2, tto twice, p 2 together, k 1, p 1, k 4, tto twice, p 2 together, k 2. Repeat.

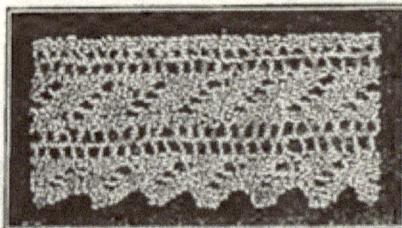

1 oz. silk No. 300 makes 3 yds. above pattern.
1 oz. silk No. 500 makes 5 yds. 7 inches above pattern.

FIG. 86.

RULE 87.

LACE EDGING. (Fig. 87.)

Cast on 10 stitches, knit across plain. 1st row, k 2, tto twice, p 2 together, k 1, tto twice, n, tto twice, n, k 1.——2d row, k 2, k 1 loop, p 1 loop, k 1, k 1 loop, p 1 loop, k 1, tto twice, p 2 together, k 2.——3d row, k 2, tto twice, p 2 together, k 3, tto twice, n, tto twice, n, k 1.—— 4th row, k 2, k 1 loop, p 1 loop, k 1, k 1 loop, p 1 loop, k 3, tto twice, p 2 together, k 2.——5th row, k 2, tto twice, p 2 together, k 5, tto twice, n, tto twice, n, k 1.——6th row, k 2, k 1 loop, p 1 loop, k 1, k 1 loop, p 1 loop, k 5, tto twice, p 2 together, k 2.—— 7th row, k 2, tto twice, p 2 together, k 7, tto twice, n, tto twice, n, k 1.—— 8th row, k 2, k 1 loop, p 1

FIG. 87.

loop, k 1, k 1 loop, p 1 loop, k 7, tto twice, p 2 together, k 2.——9th row, k 2, tto twice, p 2 together, k 14.——10th row, cast off 8, k 6, tto twice, p 2 together, k 2. Repeat.

1 oz. silk No. 300 makes 3 yds. 3 inches above pattern.
1 oz. silk No. 500 makes 5 yds. 13 inches above pattern.

RULE 88.

LACE EDGING. (Fig. 88.)

Cast on 15 stitches, knit across plain. 1st row, k 2, tto twice, p 2 together, k 1, tto twice, n, k 8.——2d row, k 9, k 1 loop, p 1 loop, k 1, tto twice, p 2 together, k 2.——3d row, k 2, tto twice, p 2 together, k 12.——4th row, k 12, tto twice, p 2 together, k 2.——5th row, k 2, tto twice, p 2 together, k 1, tto twice, n, tto twice, n, k 7.——6th row, k 8, k 1 loop, p 1 loop, k 1, k 1 loop, p 1 loop, k 1, tto twice, p 2 together, k 2.——7th row, k 2, tto twice, p 2 together, k 14.——8th row, k 14, tto twice, p 2 together, k 2.——9th row, k 2, tto twice, p 2 together, k 1, tto twice, n, tto twice, n, k 7.——

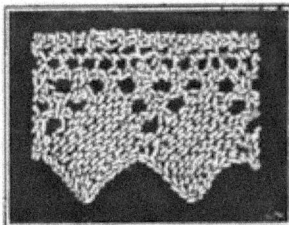

FIG. 88.

10th row, k 8, k 1 loop, p 1 loop, k 1, k 1 loop, p 1 loop, k 1, k 1 loop, p 1 loop, k 1, tto twice, p 2 together, k 2.——11th row, k 2, tto twice, p 2 together, k 17.—— 12th row, cast off to 15 stitches, k 10, tto twice, p 2 together, k 2. Repeat.

1 oz. silk No. 300 makes 2 yds. 35 inches above pattern.
1 oz. silk No. 500 makes 5 yds. 6 inches above pattern.

RULE 89.

LACE EDGING. (Fig. 89.)

Cast on 18 stitches, knit across plain. 1st row, s 1, k 2, tto twice, p 2 together, k 5, n, tto, k 3, tto, k 3.——2d and every alternate row, knit plain until there are only 5 stitches left, then tto twice, p 2 together, k 2.——3d row, s 1, k 2, tto twice, p 2 together, k 4, n, tto, k 5, tto, k 3 ——5th row, s 1, k 2, tto twice, p 2 together, k 3 n, tto, k 1, n, tto, k 1, tto, n, k 1, tto, k 3.——7th row, s 1, k 2, tto twice, p 2 together, k 2, n, tto, k 1, n, tto, k 3, tto, n, k 1, tto, k 3 ——9th row, s 1, k 2, tto twice, p 2 together, k 1, n, tto, n, k 1, tto, k 5, tto, n, k 1, tto, k 3.——11th row, s 1, k 2, tto twice, p 2 together, k 2, tto, n, k 1, n, tto, n, n, tto, k 1, n, tto, k 1, n, tto, k 3.——13th row, s 1, k 2, tto twice, p 2 together, k 3, tto, n, k 1, tto, n, k 1, n, tto, k 1 n, tto, n, k 2.——15th row, s 1, k 2, tto twice, p 2 together, k 4, tto, n, k 1, tto, s 1, n, pass s over, tto, k 1, n, tto, n, k 2.——17th row, s 1, k 2, tto twice, p 2 together, k 5, tto, n, k 3, n, tto, n, k 2.——19th row, s 1, k 2, tto twice, p 2 together, k 6, tto, n, k 1, n, tto, n, k 2.——21st row, s 1, k 2, tto twice, p 2 together, k 7, tto, s 1, n, pass s over, tto, n, k 2. Repeat

FIG. 89.

1 oz silk No. 300 makes 1 yd. 28 inches above pattern.

1 oz. silk No. 500 makes 2 yds. 34 inches above pattern.

—

RULE 90.

LACE EDGING. (Fig. 90.)

Cast on 18 stitches, knit across plain. 1st row, k 2, tto, s and b, tto, s and b, k 4, tto, s 1, n, pass s over, tto, n, tto, k 1, k 2 together crossed. —— 2d row, s 1, k 6, n, k 3, p 1, k 1, p 1, k 2.——3d row, k 2, tto, s and b, tto, s and b, k 3, tto twice, p 3, tto, n, tto, k 2.——4th row, s 1, k 8, n, k 2, p 1, k 1, p 1, k 2 ——5th row, k 2, tto, s and b, tto, s and b, k 2, tto, s 1, n, pass s over, tto thrice, n, tto, n, tto, k 2. —— 6th row, s 1, k 5, in the three loops (formed by tto thrice in previous row) k 1, p 1 and k 1, k 1, p 1, n, k 1, p 1, k 1, p 1, k 2 —— 7th row, k 2, tto, s and b, tto, s and b, k 1, tto, k 7, tto, n, tto, k 2. —— 8th row, s 1, k 4, p 7, k 3, p 1, k 1, p 1, k 2.——9th row, k 2, tto, s and b, tto, s and b, k 2, tto, n, k 3, n, tto, n, tto, k 1, k 2 together crossed.——10th row, s 1, k 4, p 5, k 4, p 1, k 1, p 1, k 2.——11th row, k 2, tto, s and b, tto, s and b, k 3, tto, n, k 1, n, tto, n, tto, k 1, k 2 together crossed. ——12th row, s 1, k 4, p 3, k 5, p 1, k 1, p 1, k 2. Repeat.

FIG. 90.

1 oz. silk No. 300 makes 2 yds. 9 inches above pattern.

1 oz. silk No. 500 makes 3 yds. 33 inches above pattern.